W9-CTP-300

Fast Ideas
for
Busy Teachers

150 Productive Activities for Teachers, Substitutes and Parents

by Greta Barclay Lipson, Ed.D.

illustrated by Susan Kropa

Cover by Susan Kropa

Copyright © Good Apple, Inc., 1989

ISBN No. 0-86653-504-7

Good Apple
A Division of Frank Schaffer Publications, Inc.
23740 Hawthorne Boulevard
Torrance, CA 90505-5927

Dedicated to the Barclay-Lipson Clan and Friends

To the professional eaters and the big talkers.
To the countless family festivities—
Get togethers, story fests, howlers,
Bountiful and amplitudinous good times—
Where we have always convened laughing and clapping
As our own very best raucous audience.
To good times,
To good health,
To good loving!

GA1082

Contents

GA1082

GA1082

Personal Note to the Teacher

Writing for teachers is a strange and wonderful pursuit. (The writing is a love-hate thing, but the research is pure fascination.) The ideas in this book started with teachers in classrooms, with undergrads and grad students, with student teachers and often in an atmosphere of pure spontaneity. But it is emphatically in the classrooms—with real, living, breathing students—where ideas are generated. So it starts—"out there" where the ideas begin and grow and finally, insistently demand to be written down and shared. This book has been years in coming.

Even after a collection of this kind is written, it can only be fully realized in the hands of teachers who interpret, re-create, and implement the ideas in their own ways. I know it happens, and sometimes, if I am lucky, I witness this "teaching art" or hear about the reinvention of an idea. It becomes a variation on a theme, a view from a distant planet, and a strategy to make it accessible to different kinds of students. My regret is in not being able to witness the event oftener. Not only is it exciting but it exceeds, by far, anything visualized at its inception. The interpretation of ideas by other teachers is one of the greater rewards of this kind of writing.

All of this is preliminary to saying—use this book of activities in any way that suits your particular style. If an activity suggests a solo student effort and you see it as a smashing whole class enterprise—then go ahead. You are the best judge of what will work for you and what won't. Expand an idea, take a portion of it, use it as a springboard. Above all, endow the material with your own vision and vitality.

I am speaking to the creative process as manifested in a great many teachers who never think of themselves in extravagant terms. But they should. Teachers who scout around in search of innovative ideas are a special breed who are, themselves, captivated by information, unsolved problems, and the endless amazing circuitry inside the head. The drive is part of the energy-charge of teaching and a grand metaphor for the profession.

So use what you can in the book. Be shamelessly derivative (that's what art is all about)! And remember—none of it is sacred. I only wish I could be there to record the permutations!

GA1082

How This Book Can Help You

Have you ever:

- Wanted to energize the last moments of a tired Friday afternoon?

- Needed an exciting, educational activity for your pupils that would take 10, 15 or 30 minutes?

- Wanted a warm experience to enhance the sense of community in your classroom?

- Looked for a skills activity to make your pupils wild with enthusiasm?

- Needed comic relief to follow the fatigue of a tough lesson?

- Been eager to show your pupils to their best advantage while being observed?

- Needed a concept so versatile that it generates numerous spin-off activities?

- Tried to make magic for a teachable moment?

- Wanted some great rainy day activities?

- Searched for a compendium of interesting skills exercises for all occasions?

Be honest! We have all had these immediate needs if we have worked with children. For that reason we are gratified to bring you these dependable, timeless ideas.

You will find an activity for every mood, be it quiet, active or in-between. There are activities for whole class participation, for groups, partnerships, and for solo endeavors. Use these versatile ideas for oral and/or written expression.

Some of the suggestions on the following pages are instant winners. Some may need a little time and preparation, but all are workable and have been field tested with real children. Adapt these activities to your own students and your collective

GA1082

Acronyms: Time-Savers

An acronym is a word that is formed by using the beginning letters of a series of words. To be a true acronym, as distinguished from an initialism, or an abbreviation, it must be a pronounceable word. Acronyms were made up as a way of saving time and space in writing and speaking, just as it is easier to use an initialism like TGIF to say "Thank goodness it's Friday." People try to develop tricky sounding acronyms which the public is more likely to remember, and in doing so may take liberties with the words that are used. One of the first and most famous acronyms is *radar*. Look that one up in the dictionary to find out what it stands for! Some others are

MASH:	Mobile Army Surgical Hospitals
NOW:	National Organization for Women
SADD:	Students Against Drunk Driving
SKOTEYS:	Spoiled Kids of the Eighties
YUPPIES:	Young Urban Professionals
GLITCH:	Goblin Loose in the Computer Hut
BADD:	Bostonians Against Disability Discrimination

Try your hand at naming an organization and giving it an acronym that is clever and is fun to remember. Perhaps you can start backwards and make the expanded name fit the acronym. It will be easier if your acronym is short. You may use a word that is already in the language like NOW, or you may make up a new word.

There are reference books that explain acronyms, initialisms, and abbreviations which are updated yearly. See GALE RESEARCH CO., 835 Penobscot Building, Detroit, Michigan 48226.

GA1082

Acrostic: Say It Vertically and Horizontally

An acrostic is a series of words (sometimes of equal length) arranged so that the whole piece can be read vertically or horizontally. It may be a puzzle, a poem, or a statement. In this acrostic the title of the topic is printed vertically letter by letter. Each letter is used to begin a phrase or sentence which describes the topic.

1. Think of a topic that will make a good title. Short titles work best: pizza, fishing, musician, race car, sweethearts, baby sister, parents, football, collision, hockey, fashion, roller coaster.
2. Write the title of your acrostic across your paper.
3. Take every letter from your title and write it vertically on your paper. If you are using more than one word, skip a line between words.
4. Now you must describe your topic. This is the hard part so take your time. Your phrase or sentence must begin with the letter you have placed on the side. On a separate piece of paper, write as many colorful sentences or phrases as you can think of that tell something about your subject.

Example:

HOMEWORK
Hours of sweating
Over books and papers
Making every effort to understand
Everything that's assigned.
Wondering if I can stay awake
Overnight to finish the job.
Relieved to close the books—
Knowledge is a dangerous thing!

Try this:

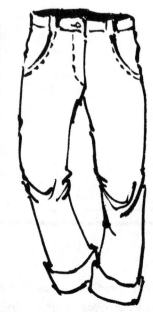

BLUE JEANS

B _____

L _____

U _____

E _____

J _____

E _____

A _____

N _____

S _____

Read yours aloud to the class!

GA1082

Alliteration

When similar beginning sounds (usually consonants) are used in two or more words close together, we get the effect of alliteration. It can be challenging to construct alliterative thoughts and is always pleasing to the ear for young and old alike. Here is an early alliterative jingle from Mother Goose.

Thomas A. Tattamus took two T's,

To tie two tups to two tall trees,

To frighten the terrible Thomas A. Tattamus!

Tell me how many T's there are in THAT.

1. In order to make your alliterative sentences sensible, you may use three beginning alliterations and finish the sentence with other consonants.

   Example: Farmers fight frogs in their creeks.

   Tina tosses a terrific football!

2. If you can stretch further, make every word in the phrase start with the same consonant.

   Example: Rugged Rachel runs a rough, rigorous race,

   Pamela the pilot prefers powerful, precision planes.

   Bold Benny bakes big brown bagels back at his brother's bustling bakery!

How far can you stretch a sentence and still create one that makes sense? Try writing alliterative sentences using all the consonants in the alphabet.

┌─ WORK SPACE ━━━━━━━━

RUGGED RACHEL
RUNNING RIGOROUSLY

GA1082

Alphabet Poetry

Using the familiar ABC's, poet Paul West has given us "Alphabet Poetry." The traditional arrangement of the ABC's provides the framework for the creative writer who chooses a particular topic, selects words to capture that topic, and arranges the words in alphabetical order. There is no rule about the number of words to place on one line. Don't use the first words that occur to you. Search for strong, colorful words. Some very pleasing free verse can be produced in this way. Take advantage of a broad range of categories which come to mind and focus on many of the things that are common or unusual in our environment.

Some examples would be food, sports, animals, exams, fashion, music, school.

When you come to x or z you may use poetic license and form a word that has the sound of the letter in it as in *xceptional* or *xcellent*. You may also create a nonsense word if you are in trouble—but only as a last resort. Remember, the production must make sense.

Shoes

Accents, big
clumsy, dirty, elegant
fashionable, grand heels
interesting
jive, kinky
loafers, messy,
nifty, old, pointy
queer
ridiculous sneakers
toes up
vamps wide
xceptional, yellow
zany.

4

Area Codes and Time Zones

The map on this page and the list on the following pages will help you find area codes. If you cannot find an area code you need, call your operator for help.

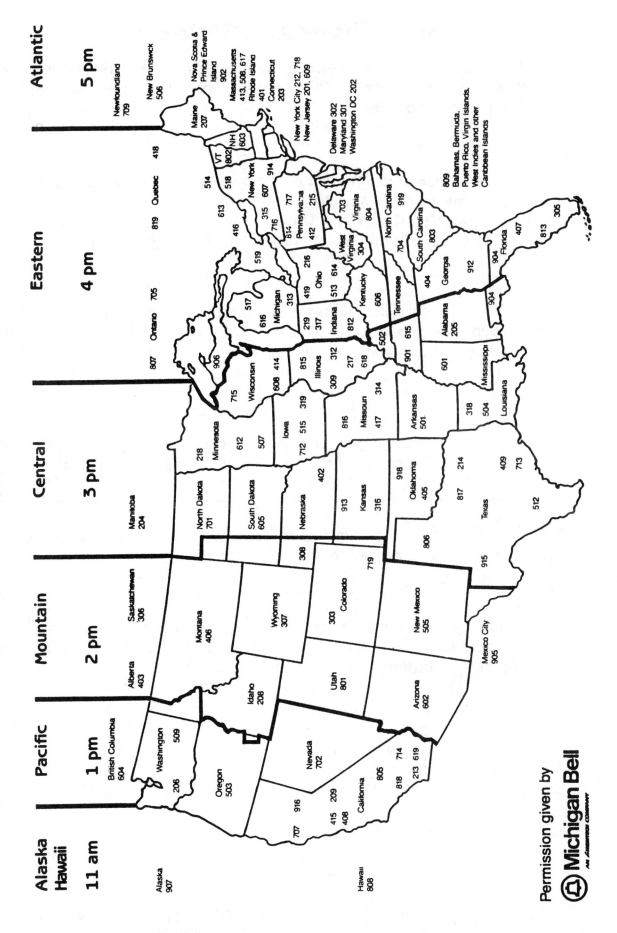

5

Permission given by
Michigan Bell
An Ameritech Company

GA1082

Area Codes and Time Zones

1. Jack is visiting his aunt in Chicago and decides to call his Mom in Omaha (Nebraska). It is 9:45 a.m. Chicago time when Jack calls. What time does Jack's mother's clock read?

   _____

2. Daylight saving time is time that is one hour later than standard time. Daylight saving time was introduced to give an hour more of daylight at the end of the usual working day. It is 1:00 p.m. Eastern standard time. What time is it in California if California has enacted daylight saving time?

   _____

3. A salesman in Louisville, Kentucky, decides to call clients in Manitoba, Canada, and Alberta, Canada. It is 10:50 a.m. in Louisville, and he must complete his calls before 10:00 a.m. in his clients' time zones. Which province should he call first?

   _____

4. You depart the Maine airport at 3:00 p.m. Eastern standard time for a three-hour flight to California. What time is it in California when you arrive?

   _____

5. You wish to call a friend in Puerto Rico. What is the area code you must dial? Search for the answer to this one.

   _____

6. Draw five clocks—one for each time zone showing the correct time across the country for Atlantic time, Eastern, Central, Mountain, and Pacific. Start at 5:00 p.m. Atlantic time.

GA1082

Attention: Shun Tion

Attention—calling all stations to action and cooperation!

A most amazing language exercise is making a list of all the words the class can think of that end with "tion." Everyone in class participates as the list grows on the chalkboard. At the same time, students at their seats will copy the original list. At the end of the day transcribe this list onto a piece of white butcher paper to be posted in the room. The next day anyone who has read, heard, or thought up more "tion" words may add them to the list in magic marker.

The list will go on for days—so just keep making additions. Perhaps somebody, somewhere knows exactly how many "tion" words there are in the English language. But however long the list becomes, it will serve as class recreation and instruction not to mention the fatal attraction in its creation!

Beware of duplications!

GA1082

Backwards: Sdrawkcab Language

When in Sdrawkcab, do as the Sdrawkcab do!

1. My name is <u>Kram Retrac</u>.

2. I was born in the month of <u>Rebotco</u>.

3. My <u>seye</u> are <u>eulb</u>.

4. I am <u>neetriht</u> years <u>dlo</u> and <u>evif</u> <u>toof</u> <u>llat</u>.

5. I attend <u>Drof Loohcs</u> and my teacher's name is <u>Rm. Trebla Namssork</u>.

6. I live on <u>Elpam Eva</u>, in the <u>ytic</u> of <u>Tiorted</u> in <u>Acirema</u>.

7. My best <u>dneirf</u> is named <u>Kire Yalcrab</u>.

8. The <u>trops</u> I enjoy most is <u>flog</u>.

9. My favorite <u>sdoof</u> are <u>nrocpop</u> and <u>azzip</u>.

10. The funniest <u>gnos</u> I ever heard is "<u>Eeknay Eldood Ydnad</u>."

11. I like to wear <u>eulb</u> <u>snaej</u>.

12. My favorite subject in <u>loohcs</u> is <u>laicos</u> <u>seiduts</u>.

13. I like to <u>daer</u>. A great <u>koob</u> is *<u>Rebbulb</u>*.

When you have translated this form, make out a similar form with your personal information. Include any additional information which might be important in Sdrawkcab. Be careful! Your form will be read by srehcaet. Show them you can lleps in their language.

GA1082

Bagel Mania: the Dig

You are a member of an archeological team itemizing the artifacts of an ancient culture. You keep coming across a petrified object called a bagel. You are sure it has some kind of special significance because of the many sites where bagels have been found. There is no mention of these objects in the classical literature.

As a scholar and a researcher, you have been asked to speculate on the uses of these bagels; what these objects are; what they mean; how they were used; and how it happens that they did not deteriorate. Please write your official report for the Intellectual Properties Office, to the attention of Professor Diggor O'Dell, Chief Administrator. Give your rank and Social Security number, and the geographical location of your excavation. Don't forget the day, date, and century.

Some questions to include: (Give specific answers.)
1. Is this object or artifact a discovery from the Plastic Age, or some other age still unnamed?

2. In what places were the bagels found?

3. With what other objects were the bagels associated?

4. Was there an association with cooking fires or tools?

For the Teacher

Help students really <u>stretch</u> with specific responses. Were the bagels found in dwellings, schools, temples, places of commerce? Were bagels the work of folk artists? Did they grow in the ground? Did they fall from the sky like fragmented meteors? Were they objects of warfare? Were they venerated as religious objects?

GA1082

Banners and Crests

A flag is a symbol of a country. In the same way a banner may stand for a team, a school, an organization, or a special group of people. Think about a colorful and interesting design for a class banner which captures the spirit of your unique class. Items to consider for your banner may be the school name, the teacher's name, a motto, a mascot, the interests or accomplishments of the group. Decide about colors and symbols by brainstorming. You may also develop your own banner by making these decisions independently and creating your own design. Use these banners to display around the room. Combine the best qualities of those on display, by class vote, and produce an official banner of the year for your class!

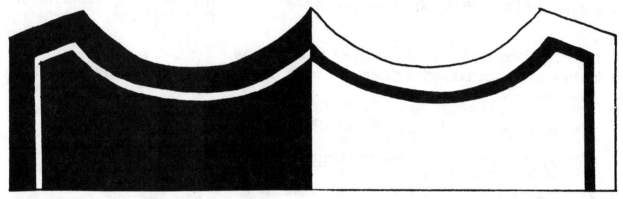

A family banner or crest represents the same kind of group expression. How would you represent your family on a crest? Remember everybody including the cats, dogs and other pets at home. If your folks love to eat, you might want to draw a knife and fork. If the family enjoys travel, include the family car. Anything will work, such as Grandpa's hammer, your mother's walking shoes or other activities of shared interest.

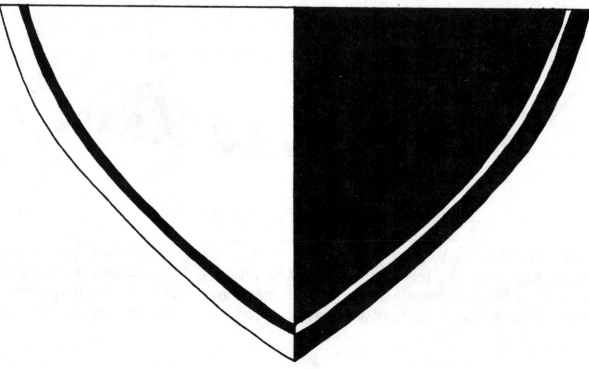

GA1082

Beauty

Write the following quotes on the chalkboard or duplicate them for each student. Add to them any other expressions that you can remember that make a comment on beauty. Clarify the meaning of each statement and discuss the implications of each. Can the statements be contradictory?

- Beauty is in the eye of the beholder.

- Beauty as we feel it is something indescribable.

- Beauty is only skin deep.

- What is beautiful is invisible to the eye.

- Beauty in nature is poetry for the soul.

- Beauty can pierce one like a pain.

- Beauty without grace is the hook without the bait.

- Beauty is everlasting.

- Beauty that's external fades.

- Beauty that's internal endures.

Extend the concept of beauty beyond personal appearance. Start a booklet in class in which each member of the room will contribute, including the teacher. The title of the book will be "Beauty is . . . ." For example:

Teacher: Beauty is a class full of hard-working students.

Students: . . . carnival lights sparkling at the edge of my town.

        . . . a 10-speed bike on Christmas morning.

        . . . a closed school building during summer vacation.

        . . . the winter beach looking like a moonscape.

        . . . a father looking at his infant baby.

        . . . a plump juicy hot dog crackling over hot charcoal.

        . . . a home run.

Whatever you consider to be beautiful, expressed in the best way you know how, is acceptable for a class book with illustrations.

GA1082

Be a Famous Person

Think about a famous person or popular hero you have read about or heard about in science, art, music, theater, politics, literature, sports, business, labor. Your person may be in the past or present as long as you would enjoy knowing more about this outstanding individual.

Read all you can about the life and accomplishments of your celebrity. You should write down some biographical facts that you think people should know about. Give some of these facts to the teacher in the form of questions so that she can distribute them to members of the class. The date and place of birth is important to establish the period during which the famous person lived.

On the appointed Friday come to class wearing a name card to identify your famous person immediately. You should also be dressed up in some way to suggest the character you are playing. Sit on a platform or stool in front of the class and answer class questions as if you were the famous person. Capture the spirit and guts of your celebrity. If someone should ask a question and you don't have the information—make up an answer that is convincing and reasonable for your character.

There should be a time limit for the question period. You may then want to introduce some additional facts about your celebrity which were not discussed. That is also the time to reveal which of your answers were fiction and were not based on the facts! Why did you decide to be this particular man or woman? What was so fascinating about your choice?

ELIZABETH BLACKWELL, M.D.
1821-1910

Answer in the first person, as follows:

Question: Why was it so difficult for you to get into medical school?

Elizabeth Blackwell: Because women were not allowed entrance into medical schools when I applied.

Question: Then why didn't you drop out when they did so many things to humiliate you?

Blackwell: Because I knew I was smart enough to become a doctor, and I was determined not to let anything stop me.

GA1082

Big Dilemma: Trapped in the Past

I am in a lot of trouble. I just hope that someone will read this and be able to rescue me from the stockade where I am imprisoned. I don't know who they are, but they do speak a kind of English. They have asked me who I am, where I come from and how I got here. When I answer they think I am lying. They don't understand the technology of the modern world we live in. I'm having trouble explaining it so that these primitive people will understand. And that's my big problem. They have made me repeat my story every day to different people. They claim that if I can't make them believe the stories of my world soon, they will burn me as a witch. How would you explain the modern inventions of our world without sounding crazy? Help me, please! This is what I have told them:

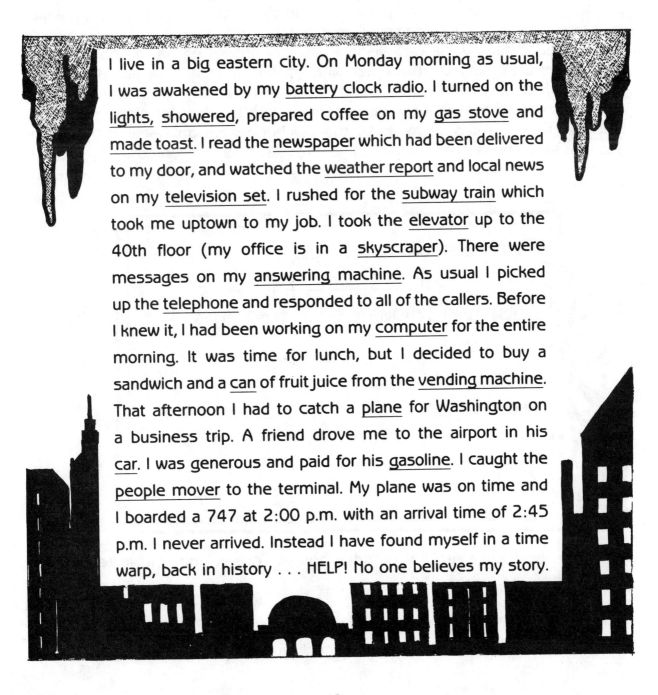

I live in a big eastern city. On Monday morning as usual, I was awakened by my battery clock radio. I turned on the lights, showered, prepared coffee on my gas stove and made toast. I read the newspaper which had been delivered to my door, and watched the weather report and local news on my television set. I rushed for the subway train which took me uptown to my job. I took the elevator up to the 40th floor (my office is in a skyscraper). There were messages on my answering machine. As usual I picked up the telephone and responded to all of the callers. Before I knew it, I had been working on my computer for the entire morning. It was time for lunch, but I decided to buy a sandwich and a can of fruit juice from the vending machine. That afternoon I had to catch a plane for Washington on a business trip. A friend drove me to the airport in his car. I was generous and paid for his gasoline. I caught the people mover to the terminal. My plane was on time and I boarded a 747 at 2:00 p.m. with an arrival time of 2:45 p.m. I never arrived. Instead I have found myself in a time warp, back in history . . . HELP! No one believes my story.

13

GA1082

Birthday Book

Everybody has a birthday, and everybody knows about the good feelings we have when our special day comes around once a year. We remember on this day that every single human being is a very unique person indeed, for there are no two people in the world who are exactly alike. Each of us in our own way has something to give the world that no one else can. Each of us is a valuable human being. So on our birthdays, we celebrate our personal importance and the wonder of our membership in the whole human race. Birthdays are celebrated in different ways. Many people have parties to which they invite their friends, some have a family celebration, while others especially enjoy celebrating in school and receiving greetings and special attention from teacher and classmates alike.

Each student will contribute a page to a Birthday Book for the birthday person. Use large colored construction paper. On one side write a signed greeting which says something really good and positive about the birthday person. (Spelling words may be requested by the well-wishers and can be written on the board. These also act as catalysts.) On the other side of the paper draw a birthday picture which can include all of the things we associate with birthday celebrations. Maintain a wide margin to the left of these greeting cards to allow for staples and tape binding. The cover can be made by the teacher, with a gold seal in the corner and crossed ribbons. These are often kept for years as mementos.

COVER

```
HAPPY BIRTHDAY TO_____

DAY AND DATE_____

BEST WISHES FROM THE CLASS IN ROOM _____

TEACHER _____

SCHOOL NAME _____

BEST WISHES ON YOUR _____ BIRTHDAY!
```

See the next page for "My Birthday Song." Consult your music teacher for the tune.

Greta Lipson. *It's a Special Day*. Carthage, Illinois: Good Apple, Inc., 1978.

Birthday Song

Sweet cake and Ice cream can-dles to blow Pre-sents and sun-shine
Friends that I know Peo-ple I care for shar-ing this way are
sing-ing and laugh-ing on my spe-cial day Yes we a- gree
Yes, we a- gree come to my birth-day and cel-e-brate me.

There's only one
You surely can see
That one and only
Little old me.

Smiling and happy
Proud that I am
A singular person
In all of the land.

Yes, we agree
Yes, we agree
Come to my birthday
And celebrate me.

Especially good
Incredibly fine
I try to be this
Most of the time.

Sing on my birthday,
Celebrate me!
A good day—My best day,
We all will agree!

Yes, we agree
Yes, we agree
Come to my birthday
And celebrate me.

Greta Lipson, Music by Harriet Goldman. *It's a Special Day*. Carthage, Illinois:
Good Apple, Inc., 1978.

15

GA1082

Birthday Trivia

Put this birthday information together and make your own natal day profile!

Happy Horoscopes

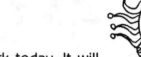

ARIES (March 21-April 19)

You will enjoy yourself with your friends today. Your friends and family will want to be with you and share your happy face. A Libra person will come to you for help. You will be kind, as always, and do what you can.

TAURUS (April 20-May 20)

You will be doing a lot of hard work today. It will please you because you will do such an excellent job. Some people will want to ask you how you are able to work so well alone. An Aquarius wants to be your friend.

GEMINI (May 21-June 20)

A Capricorn person will be in your life today just for fun. You will enjoy really good times during and after school. People think you know how to share and this will put everyone around you in a fine mood.

CANCER (June 21-July 22)

Today is a day for getting things cleaned up and put in order. You set a good example for your friends and they all want to do the same thing. You will feel very proud of a Scorpio's compliment.

LEO (July 23-Aug. 22)

You will have a chance to show your friends what it really means to be a good sport. You may lose at a game today, but you have a smile on your face. A Taurus admires you.

VIRGO (Aug. 23-Sept. 22)

You may earn a treat today for being very courteous. A Leo and Aries will say some wonderful things to you for being such a good citizen. You find it very easy to work well with people, and others try hard to be like you.

GA1082

LIBRA (Sept. 23-Oct. 22)

Everything will be brighter today. You must make a decision, and you will use good common sense. Like always, you will think carefully about things before you act. A Virgo thinks you are a very special person.

SCORPIO (Oct. 23-Nov. 21)

There will be a chance to work with other people today. You will attract attention because you really understand about cooperation. A Pisces will tell others how fine you are.

SAGITTARIUS (Nov. 22-Dec. 21)

Today you will learn something by teaching someone else. You are very understanding and others listen to you. Everyone knows how helpful you are, and they enjoy being with you. A Virgo person admires you secretly.

CAPRICORN (Dec. 22-Jan. 19)

You will have more freedom today and will make very good use of your spare time. You do not waste anything and you are a good example for a Pisces who thinks you are great. Your good ideas always surprise people.

AQUARIUS (Jan. 20-Feb. 18)

Today will be another day when you make other people happy. You always have a pleasant greeting and a nice word for everyone. You understand how to be considerate of other people's feelings. A Gemini would like to get to know you better.

PISCES (Feb. 19-March 20)

You give your friends a chance to express themselves. Today you will show others how easy it is to do this while you are having a serious talk. You respect people and they admire you for your attitude. A Sagittarius tries to act just like you.

GA1082

Use the number of your birth month to find your birthstone, flower and color.

Months
1. January
2. February
3. March
4. April
5. May
6. June
7. July
8. August
9. September
10. October
11. November
12. December

Birthstones and Their Meanings
1. garnet—constancy
2. amethyst—sincerity
3. aquamarine—courage
4. diamond—innocence
5. emerald—love, success
6. moonstone, pearl—health
7. ruby—contentment
8. peridot—happiness
9. sapphire—clear thinking
10. opal—hope
11. topaz—fidelity
12. turquoise—prosperity

Flowers
1. carnation
2. violet
3. daffodil
4. sweet pea
5. lily of the valley
6. rose
7. water lily
8. gladiolus
9. morning glory
10. calendula
11. chrysanthemum
12. holly

Colors
1. black and white
2. deep blue
3. gray or silver
4. yellow
5. lavender or lilac
6. pink or rose
7. sky blue
8. deep green
9. orange or gold
10. brown
11. purple
12. red

GA1082

Birthday Zodiac Signs
What Is Your Sign?

Astrology is not a science and should not be mistaken for astronomy, which is the scientific study of the heavenly bodies and their motions. Though astrology is not a science it, too, is the study of the sun, moon, planets and stars.

Astrology is thousands of years old and is based upon the ancient idea that the future of each person can be predicted by his birth sign. Each person is born under one of the twelve signs of the zodiac. Character and development are supposed to be influenced by the heavenly bodies.

The zodiac is an imaginary belt among the stars. It is the portion of the sky through which the sun, moon and planets move from east to west. Nearly all the groups of stars in the zodiac are named after animals.

Even though we may not believe in astrology, it is entertaining to find our signs in the zodiac and look at a horoscope to tell our fortunes. A horoscope is a chart showing the influences of the stars on the personalities and lives of people.

Write down the month and day of your birthday and then find your birth sign. Every newspaper has a daily horoscope that predicts the kind of day you will have.

Signs of the Zodiac

Name	Dates
Aries the Ram	March 21-April 19
Taurus the Bull	April 20-May 20
Gemini the Twins	May 21-June 20
Cancer the Crab	June 21-July 22
Leo the Lion	July 23-August 22
Virgo the Virgin	August 23-September 22
Libra the Balance	September 23-October 22
Scorpio the Scorpion	October 23-November 21
Sagittarius the Archer	November 22-December 21
Capricorn the Goat	December 22-January 19
Aquarius the Water Bearer	January 20-February 18
Pisces the Fishes	February 19-March 20

The signs of the zodiac were named by the ancient Greeks. These names represent twelve constellations of stars, each taken for astrological purposes and represented by a different symbol. Depending upon one's birth date, each person is thought to be born under a different sign.

GA1082

Bulwer-Lytton: Fiction Contest

Many teachers and students are familiar with the opening sentence of a novel published in 1830 written by Bulwer-Lytton. That first sentence reads: "It was a dark and stormy night," and the sentence drones on forever, finally ending with a description of the wind as "fiercely agitating the scanty flame of the lamps." That long sentence was considered to be so excruciatingly awful that it haunts us today and is still good for laughs.

Because this is true, every year there is a national Bulwer-Lytton Fiction Contest, which is sponsored by Dr. Scott Rice, a professor of English at San Jose State University in California. The task of the contest entrants is to produce the worst, incredibly long opening sentence for a novel. These entries are judged by writers, and the "best of the worst" wins the contest. In 1987 there were 10,000 entries. Professor Scott claims that you must know how to write well in order to recognize bad writing and imitate it!

1. Summon up your worst writing skills and produce one single sentence which you think is long enough and bad enough to send in to the contest—or simply produce one very long and strange sentence for the opening of a novel which you think would capture the interest of your readers!
2. You might even select a wildly romantic pen name as the author of your sentence. A pen name (called a "nom de plume" in French) is used to conceal the author's true identity.
3. It would be interesting for a small group of students to compose one letter to Dr. Scott requesting information about the Bulwer-Lytton Fiction Contest.

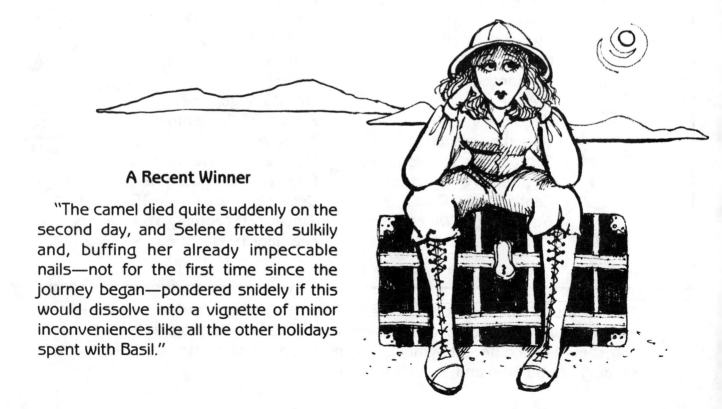

A Recent Winner

"The camel died quite suddenly on the second day, and Selene fretted sulkily and, buffing her already impeccable nails—not for the first time since the journey began—pondered snidely if this would dissolve into a vignette of minor inconveniences like all the other holidays spent with Basil."

GA1082

 # Cartoon Consonants

In the left column are titles of popular comic strips. The right column is mismatched. In order to identify the strips, you must fill in the missing consonants and match them with the left column. The vowels which appear are the only clues. Take your time! How many can you solve? How many of these syndicated strips can be found in your daily or Sunday paper?

1. DOONESBURY   (_ o _ _ e _   _ o _ a _)

2. DICK TRACY   (_ _ o _ _ i e)

3. SUPERMAN   (_ e e _ _ e   _ a i _ e _)

4. POGO   (_ o _ _ i)

5. BEETLE BAILEY   (_ i _ _   _ _ a _ _)

6. MARMADUKE   (_ e a _ u _ _)

7. PEANUTS   (_ a _ _ a _ u _ e)

8. HAGAR THE HORRIBLE (_ i _ a _ _   o _   i _)

9. NANCY   (_ _ e _ _ a   _ _ a _ _)

10. BRENDA STARR   (_ a _ _ _)

11. GASOLINE ALLEY   (_ a _ a _   _ _ e   _ o _ _ i _ _ e)

12. BLONDIE   (_ u _ e _ _ a _)

13. DONDI   (_ a _ o _ i _ e   A _ _ e _)

14. WIZARD OF ID   (_ o o _ e _ _ u _ _)

15. WONDER WOMAN   (_ o _ o)

Add your own favorite strips. Leave in the vowels and eliminate the consonants. Mix them up.

Cast a Movie

For this activity the teacher should read a story to the students which is rich in characterization and dramatic action. A short story is ideal. Mysteries, science fiction, adventure stories, comic or classical pieces, fairy tales, myths and fables are all good choices. Any piece of fiction that all the students have read or heard will do as well.

Ask the class to recall the characters of the story. List these on the board. It is time now for the casting director to start selecting actors for the production. The casting director has the very important job of matching up the personalities who seem suitable for the roles to be played. This is a very critical and skillful job. As the casting director, you have been given permission to hire anyone in your class, your school, your neighborhood—or anyone from stage, screen, or television. Careful casting can make the venture the smash of the year or a financial flop. Who will be your choice for each role?

****

If you were working without a story and had to cast some prototypic parts, who would you choose for the following? (Duplicate this list.)

1. comedian
2. mad scientist
3. superman/woman
4. big musical star
5. teacher
6. tough guy
7. secret agent
8. famous athlete male/female
9. soap opera actor
10. mother, father
11. TV newscaster
12. sports reporter
13. prosecuting attorney
14. coach
15. politician

16. detective
17. engineer
18. famous author
19. magician
20. farmer
21. William Shakespeare
22. dog trainer
23. dance instructor
24. long distance swimmer
25. physician
26. race car driver
27. movie producer
28. principal
29. a strong silent type—male/female
30. camp counselor

GA1082

Celebrate Me Booklet

Here is an idea for writing your auto-biography in your free time. First, design an attractive cover for this story of your life. The book should have a construction paper cover that is 8½" x 11"—folded in half. Cut a perfect hole in the upper right-hand corner of the cover, about the size of a quarter. Inside the back page of the cover, paste a picture of yourself. Close the cover and there you are—looking out a circle window!

Add a page whenever you are inspired with another idea. Every page you add to your book will have an identical hole in exactly the same place. When the book is finished, each time someone turns the page to read another interesting fact about your life, your face will be looking out at the reader!

Include facts about yourself which you consider important: your full name and nickname, your birth date and age, members of your family. Write about your best friend, the things you like to do, your favorite sport, the foods you love to eat. Be sure to include more about what you do well and self-improvements you would like to make. This is your book about yourself and you may include whatever you think is unique!

- What makes me laugh
- People I admire
- If I had three wishes
- A skill I would like to learn
- Something that makes me proud

GA1082

Choral Speaking I: Phoebe Snow Express

Action and Sound Effects

Narrator: Teacher

Conductor: Anaheim, Bath, Cucamonga
Wheels: Clickety clack, Clickety clack, Clickety clack
Train Whistle: Whoo whoo, Whoo whoo
Passengers: What a ride! What a ride!
Food Vendor: Peanuts, popcorn, soda pop
Robbers: Bang, bang bang, bang
Police: (Monotone siren) Doodah, doodah, doodah

Directions

Read the story first. There are seven parts to be assigned to different groups in this action-packed story. Each group must plan on the appropriate sound and action which it will perform. Each time the Narrator reads the name of the part(s), the group will rise as one and present the action and sound effects. Everyone will have a copy of the story and listen to the Narrator as they all read along silently. Rehearsals are definitely in order! Make any changes which make the reading more effective.

The beautiful new Phoebe Snow Express pulled out of the Long Branch station on gleaming WHEELS. People lined the platform to say good-bye to their friends and relatives on the train. There was waving and happy smiles as the CONDUCTOR called "all aboard" to the PASSENGERS in the station. The gleaming engine glistened in the sun as the TRAIN WHISTLE made its own romantic sounds. Everyone was thrilled to be on the new train and the enthusiasm could be seen on the faces of the PASSENGERS. They talked excitedly, looked out the windows and listened to the rhythm of the WHEELS as they passed through little towns and hamlets.

It was time for the CONDUCTOR to come around and collect tickets from the happy PASSENGERS. Of course, the trip wouldn't be complete without the treats carried down the aisle by the FOOD VENDOR! The PASSENGERS knew this was a very special event and when they bought goodies from the FOOD VENDOR, they acted as if they were on a picnic. The TRAIN WHISTLE could be heard again as the train careened around a curve into the mountain pass with echoes of the WHEELS bouncing off the mountainsides.

GA1082

Imagine the shock of the PASSENGERS when the connecting doors from the last train opened and in came some masked ROBBERS! The CONDUCTOR tried to keep everyone calm, as the WHEELS kept turning. The ROBBERS just passed by the PASSENGERS on their way to the baggage and mail cars. But first the ROBBERS took some refreshments from the FOOD VENDOR.

There was so much excitement that at first no one was sure if they really did hear something outside through the sound of the WHEELS and the TRAIN WHISTLE! But sure enough the brave CONDUCTOR had managed to contact the authorities, and it was indeed the sound of POLICE sirens coming closer and closer to them. When the POLICE boarded the train, everyone was happy and relieved. The CONDUCTOR felt good, the PASSENGERS were grateful, the FOOD VENDOR breathed a sigh of relief, and the POLICE were the heroes of the day! No one in the town of Long Branch had ever had such an exciting train trip. Only the ROBBERS were disappointed. The event would go down in the history of the railroad and be known forever as the story of the Phoebe Snow Express with its joyous TRAIN WHISTLE and rhythmic WHEELS.

GA1082

Choral Speaking II: The Circus

Follow the directions from "Choral Speaking I: Phoebe Snow Express." Divide into groups. Assign one sound effect to each group. Everyone reads silently as the Narrator begins. When your part is named, make your sound immediately.

Narrator—Teacher: Ask to hear the sounds of each group once before starting.

Circus: Oom papa, Oom papa
Suspense: Shiver, shiver, goose bumps!
Audience: Hip, hip, hooray
Ringmaster: Ladies and Gentlemen
Clowns: Hardy har har
Doggie: Woof, woof
Nose: Honk, honk, honk
Animal Trainer: Won-der-ful, Won-der-ful
Big Cat(s) and Lion: Meow, meow (Lower your voices)

The CIRCUS was back in town with all its excitement and hoopla! The RINGMASTER could be heard in front of the big tent as he shouted, "Come one, come all—pay your admission at the CIRCUS box office and experience the thrill of a lifetime." The crowd surged forward. Little did anyone know the SUSPENSE that awaited them.

It was a wonderful day for the AUDIENCE as they crowded into the tent to watch the wonders of the stunning CIRCUS. When the RINGMASTER bellowed, "Welcome to the CIRCUS," every eye in the AUDIENCE focused on his dazzling costume and slick top hat. The AUDIENCE listened as he introduced the acrobats, the elephants, the high wire stars and finally the funny CLOWNS. They tumbled and tripped and brought in their little DOGGIE who was the mascot of the CIRCUS. DOGGIE wore a big rubber NOSE and a red ruffle around his neck. No one could guess DOGGIE and his NOSE would play a role in the SUSPENSE that day!

Next to enter the center ring was the ANIMAL TRAINER. When he was announced by the RINGMASTER, the AUDIENCE went crazy. He was powerful with his whip

GA1082

and chair. The BIG CATS followed—slinking in on the heels of the ANIMAL TRAINER. The CIRCUS band blared. The three rings were alive with swirling colors and performers. This was the glory of the CIRCUS for the AUDIENCE. The CLOWNS cavorted; the DOGGIE danced on his back legs; the BIG CATS sat atop their wooden platforms; the ANIMAL TRAINER cracked his whip and the SUSPENSE was about to happen. With a signal the RINGMASTER quieted the AUDIENCE. The spotlights focused on the meanest BIG CAT of all. The ANIMAL TRAINER stepped forward and slowly opened the mouth of the LION. He put his head into the beast's mouth. The AUDIENCE gasped. It appeared as if the man had disappeared in the dark innards of the BIG CAT. The AUDIENCE was silent. You could cut the fear with a knife. The SUSPENSE was building. It was taking too long for the ANIMAL TRAINER to pull out his head. The CLOWNS pulled at his legs! The AUDIENCE was paralyzed. But not DOGGIE. With his big NOSE he bounded toward the BIG CAT and latched onto its big NOSE with his jaws clamped tightly. The BIG CAT let out a howl and tossed up the head of the ANIMAL TRAINER. The AUDIENCE clapped and shouted for the little hero. The smart DOGGIE took a bow as his rubber NOSE bobbled on his face; the CLOWNS turned somersaults; the RINGMASTER threw kisses; the CIRCUS band played louder than ever. The ANIMAL TRAINER fainted dead away and the SUSPENSE was over. What a great day at the CIRCUS!

27

Choral Speaking III: Your Production

Now that you have tried two choral speaking efforts ("Phoebe Snow Express" and "The Circus"), it is time for you to write a script of your own! Here is what you do. Think of a place where there are many interesting sounds. Think of the effective sounds your choral speakers can use as the narrator tells the story; think of a brief short story that has a beginning, middle, and ending. The final test is trying it out with the class. Don't make it too long or complicated in your first try.

Think about:

1. A place with interesting sounds is _____
   (This could even be your Main Street.)

2. Some good characters or parts to introduce would be _____

   _____

   _____

   (Think of at least five for starters.)

3. Some funny sounds for things or characters would be _____

   _____

4. This story is about _____

   The title is_____
   Now write a beginning, a middle, and an ending. Try writing a short paragraph for your first attempt. Take your time to rewrite and produce a smooth story.

5. At the top of your page list your five characters and the sounds they will make.

   For example: Hunter: Look out, look out
                  Arrows: Zing, zing, zing
                  Birds: Tweety, tweet, tweet
                  Cook: Chow down; chow down

TWEETY-TWEET-TWEET

GA1082

Circle Game Squeeze

For a really funny warm-up activity or a good laugh between classmates, the old circle game is perfect. Form a circle and hold hands. This transmits good feelings from the very beginning. There will be three people selected to be the initiators of the action that goes around the circle.

1. Initiator 1 squeezes the hand to the right. The squeeze is sent around twice to the right.

2. Initiator 1 adds a sound to the squeeze and says "Wow" with the squeeze. Send that around twice.

3. Initiator 1 sends around "Wow, wee" squeeze. That goes around twice.

4. Initiator 2 adds "Who-ha, wow, wee" squeeze. That goes around twice.

5. Initiator 2 adds a foot gesture to all the others which goes around twice.

6. Initiator 3 starts an arm gesture *going in the other direction* that goes around twice. If signals cross over going in different directions, keep it rolling!

7. The teacher or initiators may call time out to reorganize, select new initiators and start all over again. All workable ideas and innovations are welcome. Some groups can work their way through some very complicated directions!

GA1082

Clerihew: Biographical Poetry

The clerihew is a form of rhymed poetry that is named after its creator, Edmund Clerihew Bentley. It is a verse that is created from a person's first or last name, whichever is easiest to rhyme. It should tell something about the person, which makes it biographical and for that reason it usually turns out to be humorous. A clerihew consists of four lines (a quatrain) with the rhyme scheme aa, bb.

(a) Alexander Bevy
(a) Was very heavy
(b) He felt like a whale
(b) When he stepped on the scale

Try this out with the class. Select an ordinary name or the name of a famous person.

1. Write the name as you would normally: JANE KISSELBAUM
   Will *Kisselbaum* rhyme very well? If it doesn't, then go on to the next step.
2. Reverse the name: Kisselbaum, Jane
3. List the rhyming possibilities of *Jane*: rain, gain, mane, plane, reign, vain
4. Choose one rhyme word and now we have the second line:
   (a) Kisselbaum, Jane
   (a) Was extremely vain
5. Now think up some possible third lines. Again brainstorm for all the possible rhyming words for the end word in the third line.
6. Construct your fourth line and complete your clerihew. It could read:
   (a) Kisselbaum, Jane
   (a) Was extremely vain
   (b) Her life she'll pass
   (b) Before a looking glass

Try to write an autobiographical clerihew using your own name or nickname.
Use the name of a family member.
Be positive toward others, but you may poke fun at yourself!

Here's another: Gina Ferlingetti
Adores making spaghetti
She's a superior cook
Who doesn't need a book

GA1082

Come to a Party: RSVP

You have been wanting to have your good friends over to your house since September. These are people who have invited you to their houses and it's time to show your appreciation. You have finally saved enough money to buy snacks for a pay back party on a Saturday night. You talked it over with the folks and they think it's a super idea, but the planning and the shopping will be your responsibility. You want to do this a step at a time, so the party will be a success. The first thing you want to do is design a clever invitation.

1. First write out a guest list (remember your house has space limits).
2. Now use an 8½" x 11" sheet of paper (or construction paper or colorful scraps) folded like a greeting card.
3. Cut out a picture or cartoon from the newspaper to be pasted on the front cover. Make it as attractive as you can. Don't be afraid to be funny! Use magic markers, crayons, or anything for color.

4. The inside is important because you will include all the information your guests need.

Announce the party (in prose or rhyme)

Day_____ Date _____

Time_____ Brunch, lunch, supper, picnic _____

Address _____ Your name _____

Phone number _____

5. Include RSVP on the bottom of the invitation. In French this means "Respondez s'il vous plait"—Respond if you please.

Come to a Party: Menu

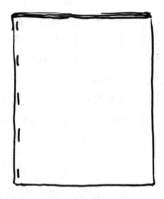

The daily newspaper stored in the classroom can be a rich source of supplementary materials and activities on a regular basis. Try stapling the paper together for easy management.

The invitations for your Saturday night party have gone out to your friends. The RSVP's have returned and you know how many guests you will be entertaining. This is the first time you have ever planned a menu so you will need the help of the supermarket advertisements in the newspaper.

1. Make out a menu.
2. Write a shopping list based upon the menu.
3. What quantities will you buy?
4. Based upon the food ads, how much will each item cost? What will be your total cost?
5. Include some other snacks suggested by the ads.

Example:

Item	Price	Quantity	Total
Hamburgers			
Hot Dogs			
Rolls			
Pickles			
Mustard			
Chips			
Dip			
Soda Pop			
Chocolate Cake			
Ice Cream			

6. What additional responsibilities or items must be considered to prepare for your guests?

GA1082

Comic Strip Dialogue

Dialogue is the conversation spoken by characters in literature. In a comic strip no quotation marks are used.

Preparation for this activity can be made in class or at home by the students.

1. Bring in the Sunday comics. Select a strip you enjoy, which has possibilities for imaginative dialogue.
2. Cut out the strip.
3. On a separate piece of paper, copy down all the characters' names and their original dialogue in the strip from frame to frame. Keep this separate for use later. It should look like this:

   Frame 1 Bobby: "What's that you're eating?"

        Dog: "It's just a bone."

   Frame 2 Bobby: "Don't look like a bone to me."

        Dog: "That's 'cause you ain't a bone specialist."

4. Cut out the dialogue balloons out of the strip without ruining the picture.
5. Paste the comic strip at the top of an 8½" x 11" sheet of paper, leaving room for writing on the lower part of the paper. Put your initials at the top, right side of the paper.

6. Pass the papers up to the front of the class to be redistributed. Each person in the class will now have a new strip to work with.
7. Look carefully at the strip and decide what the characters are saying to one another.
8. There is not enough room to make dialogue balloons over the heads of the characters so at the bottom of the paper, going frame by frame, indicate the name you have given each character. Write or print that character's conversation as you did on your own strip. You are not expected to know the names of the people.
9. Start with a volunteer who will read his invented dialogue. The originator of the strip will then read the cartoonist's dialogue that was cut out. There will probably be a big difference but don't worry about the original conversations.

   Use your own imagination for the best effect.
10. The overhead projector works well with this activity, using some of the best creative dialogue.

GA1082

Commercials: Singing and Otherwise

Every day we are bombarded with commercials on radio, television, and in the newspapers. Products and services of all kinds are peddled with songs, dances, cartoons, old people, young people, babies, dogs, cats and all creatures large and small. In a marketplace glutted with competitors, advertisers desperately want the public to buy, buy, buy their products. These commercials can be humorous, serious, educational, irritating, offensive, or downright dumb! Probably the most popular commercials are those that are humorous and entertaining. The advertisers will do anything to make you remember what they are selling.

Now it's your turn to get your revenge! Get together in groups and decide what product or service your group is going to advertise. To avoid duplications, write down your decision and hand it in to the teacher. Your group may create a singing commercial—dancing, straight talk—or any combination you choose for a presentation to the class. Everyone in the group must participate in a commercial which is not to exceed five minutes (class decision). If the excitement carries its own momentum, you may want to extend the project to the following day and plan for props, tape-recorded music, or whatever else adds flavor! It might be fun to video-tape the students if the equipment is available.

Some suggested products or services might be:

1. A weight loss clinic or product
2. Super kids for rent
3. Cereal
4. Breath mints
5. Roach killer
6. A muscle building machine
7. A cure for acne
8. Confidence lessons
9. A teacher machine for correcting papers
10. Miracle cosmetics
11. Candy
12. Nail biting prevention
13. Antihistamines
14. Hair products

GA1082

Compliments: Write a Magic Letter

One of the things we have to think about is the magic of a compliment and how wonderful it makes us feel when someone says, "You are always around when people need help," or "You played a great game," or "You're amazing" or "I'm proud that we are friends." For some reason it always seems easier to criticize, to find fault, or to take the good qualities in other people for granted. But everybody, young and old, needs a pat on the back and the admiration of others. Kind words are important for the morale, for the spirit, and they don't cost a cent. It makes you feel good about yourself to know that someone appreciates you.

Think about all of the people in your life who do things every day, every week, every month for you and others. Make a list of people who really deserve a thank-you from you.

Parent-grandparent
Teacher
Best friend
Bus driver
Custodian
Crossing guard
Teacher aid

Librarian
Schoolmate
Office secretary
Relative
Baby-sitter
Neighbor

Cafeteria person
Principal
Friend's parent-grandparent
Police officer, postal carrier
Newspaper carrier

Suggestions for starting a thank-you note:
   Because you do kind things for everyone . . .
   You understand about friendship.
   Some things are hard to say in person.
   You once did something nice I'll never forget.
   We are all lucky you are in our class.
   You bring out the best in people.
   When you work in a group, everyone cooperates.
   You know the meaning of good sportsmanship.
   Everybody enjoys your sense of humor.
   I know this will surprise you.
   After all this time I had to write and tell you . . .
   I just wanted to write a short note to let you know . . .
   I want to express my thanks to you for . . .
   It's never too late to say thanks.
   Do you know how much you help me?
   I feel good when I see you.
   You are dependable and one of the best.
   You can always be counted on.
   You're tops but you're modest anyway.

GA1082

Compound Words

Use the following list of compound words. There are two separate activities for student participation. The words can be divided by putting the beginning of the word on the board and having students identify the ending of the word from a different list distributed to the class. Raise hands, use teams, or come to the board to add the endings.

Example: On the board write fly _____ cow _____ head _____ brides _____
Students select (leaf) (boy) (ache) (maid) from a corresponding jumbled list at their desks.

Or: Partners may select any word on the list to pantomime in front of the class (with a time limit). Students at their desks will try to identify the compound word. After every skit is completed, the word should be written on the chalkboard!

Or: Students can make construction paper signs with each half of a compound word printed on it. All of the halves are placed in a box and shaken up. Ten people each pick a half word and stand in front of the class. The seated people will pick a total of ten words from the box and try to match the other half of the compound word standing. Keep picking and trying to find the other half of your word. When the words are matched they are out of circulation.

Some suggestions:

airmail	grasshopper	newsstand	suitcase
arrowhead	gumdrop	nightfall	tiptoe
bulldozer	headdress	outdoors	toadstool
butterfly	horseshoe	pancake	treetop
cowboy	icebox	paperback	understand
cupcake	jumpsuit	quarterback	wallpaper
doorman	junkyard	quicksand	waterfall
eggplant	lawman	raindrop	weekend
eyeglass	lifesaver	rattlesnake	wildlife
fishhook	meatball	shoehorn	yardstick
football	milkmaid	starfish	zookeeper

36

Concept Lyric

Some questions can be difficult to answer in just a few words. If someone were to ask, "What is loneliness or courage or friendship" it would take a lot of thought and a bit of a struggle to include everything that comes to mind when we hear these words. The solution to this is to work together on a concept verse. This activity is best done in small groups for a richer perception.

Start with: What is a _____? or What is my_____? Brainstorm all the impressions and images that are evoked when you think about a concept you want to explain or describe:

Example: What is my dog?

My best buddy
A friend in need
Dependable and caring
A sympathetic listener
A wet kisser with every hello
Playful and sweet tempered
Accepting if I'm smart or dumb
My very own heart warmer
One who loves me no matter what.

That's my dog!

Don't settle for your first impressions. Write as long a list as you can about your concept. Search for language that is like the language of poetry. You will want to include nine or ten descriptive phrases (so write out at least double that number). Don't start each phrase with the same word. Pick and choose from the best expressions. Move them around to make the entire statement most effective.

Suggested topics:
Baby brother or sister
Holidays
Courage
Friendship
Arguments
Parents
Grown-ups

A friend
Family
Team
Birthday
Parade
Circus
Generosity

Read your concept lyric to the class.

GA1082

Concrete Images

If you think about it, you know that there are certain words and sayings in our language which easily suggest pictures in our minds. Explore some of these words and sayings with your own illustrations. At the bottom of your illustrations write the words, phrases or popular sayings your concrete images represent. It is easy for a reader to put the two together. For example:

Look at these and use them to get started. Draw the word to make it suggest the meaning. Make as many choices as you can interpret. Try it with the whole class first. Draw a selection of concrete images on the chalkboard.

1. A hamburger to go
2. Time flies
3. Money to burn
4. Shaky
5. Steps
6. Drop
7. Fat
8. Skinny
9. Raining cats and dogs
10. You hit the nail on the head
11. I'm in heaven
12. Mirror, mirror on the wall
13. The walls have ears
14. Go fly a kite
15. He's a knuckle head
16. I could eat a horse
17. You drive me up the wall
18. Buzz off
19. Vine
20. A frog in my throat

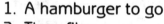

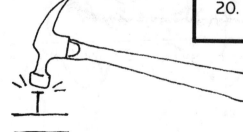

You think of some!

38

GA1082

Cookie Chant

This is a wonderful chant which can ripple its way through the entire class or be as brief as you wish. "Who Stole the Cookie from the Cookie Jar?" is a swing rhythm in 4/4 time. The students will keep time by alternately:

Clapping their hands and slapping their laps

Clapping their hands and slapping their laps

This clapping and slapping is sustained rhythmically throughout the entire chant. The rhythm must not be interrupted by *indecision*! If the class needs help with the 4/4 time, consult your friendly music teacher—or, if the class is lucky, there may be a veteran summer camper in your midst who knows how the chant works.

Begin: Have a volunteer for the first person to be named.

Group: Who stole the cookie from the cookie jar?

          Nancy stole the cookie from the cookie jar!

Nancy: Who me?

Group: Yes, you!

Nancy: Couldn't be!

Group: Then who?

(At this point, Nancy must think fast. She must choose the next person to be accused, without losing the beat.)

Nancy: Danny stole the cookie from the cookie jar!

Danny: Who me?

Group: Yes, you!

Danny: Couldn't be!

Group: Then who?

The last person to be chosen can end the chant by saying, "Oh foo." Any changes, suggestions, or variations are welcome.

GA1082

Couplets: All Kinds

Here is a chance to create rhymed couplets with the whole class. A couplet is a verse composed of two rhyming lines (the length depends upon the writer). Couplets can be simple, sophisticated, serious, funny or nonsensical.

Serious: But if the while I think on thee, dear friend (a)
            All losses are restored and sorrows end. (a)
                                        Shakespeare

Funny: His mustache looks like a bushy wig (a)
            He likes it that way 'cause his nose is big. (a)

Nonsense: Why not live sweetly among the trees (a)
            Clibbing and scarfing the zumble deez (a)

The interesting thing about using nonsense words is that it emphasizes the way our language works. We understand the proper place for a noun, a verb, or an adjective even though the words are not real English words. All the words may be nonsense in the second line, or just the last rhyming word.

Brainstorm for first lines to be put on the chalkboard. Decide on some possible rhyming words for the second line of the couplet. Compose the second line. Continue the process until there are three types of couplets on the board.

You may want to have more first lines prepared on slips of paper so that students can each pick one and write a second rhyming line individually. Each student could then write his own first line on a slip of paper and exchange it with a neighbor to be completed. Do this several times until everyone has three or four couplets. Share these orally.

Who wrote the best couplets for each classification—Serious, Funny, Nonsense? Transcribe these three winners for display.

Creative Cookery: Kid's Casserole

Your father is absolutely the best cook in America. Everybody in your family sings his praises. Whenever you ask him how he made something he always says, "I used a little of this and a little of that and a lot of imagination!"

On Friday you arrive home early from school, and there aren't any aromatic cooking smells floating out of the kitchen—instead there is a note that reads: "Dear Super Kid: I have a teacher's meeting tonight and will be home late. It's time to try your skills. It's your turn to prepare supper tonight. We shopped yesterday, and there is plenty of everything you will need to put together a delicious dinner casserole."

Pasta, Grains	Meat, Fish Chicken	Veggies	Dairy	Other
wheat	beef	potatoes	sour cream	spices
rice	chicken	tomatoes	cheese	sauces
barley	turkey	carrots	cottage cheese	gravy
buckwheat	pork	broccoli	yogurt	mustard
hominy	lamb	cabbage	milk	ketchup
macaroni	veal	green pepper	ricotta	pickle relish
tortellini	hot dogs	cauliflower	buttermilk	cornstarch
cornmeal	pepperoni	peas	margarine	flour
lasagna	corned beef	zucchini	butter	canned soup
lentils	hamburger	beans	cream cheese	tofu (bean curd)
barley	liver	celery	whipping cream	crumbs (all kinds)
spaghetti	tuna	spinach	eggs	mayonnaise
bulgur	salmon	green beans	grated cheese	croutons

There are four categories of food to choose from plus a category called "Other." You may use a maximum of ten items and a minimum of seven. You must choose at least one item from each category. Any other challenging guidelines from the class are welcome. List the items you will use; explain how you will put them together. Your recipe should be complete enough for others to follow. When you are through, give the casserole a name. If you are adventurous you may want to actually make the recipe at home and bring it in on Gourmet Day. (We just made that up.)

GA1082

From the four categories I will use _____

_____

From the "Other" category I will use _____

_____

I will prepare the casserole in this way: (chop, cube, saute, etc.)_____

Baking temperature _____° and time _____
minutes/hours

The name of my masterpiece is _____

My comments and/or problems _____

_____

_____

42

GA1082

Crystal Ball

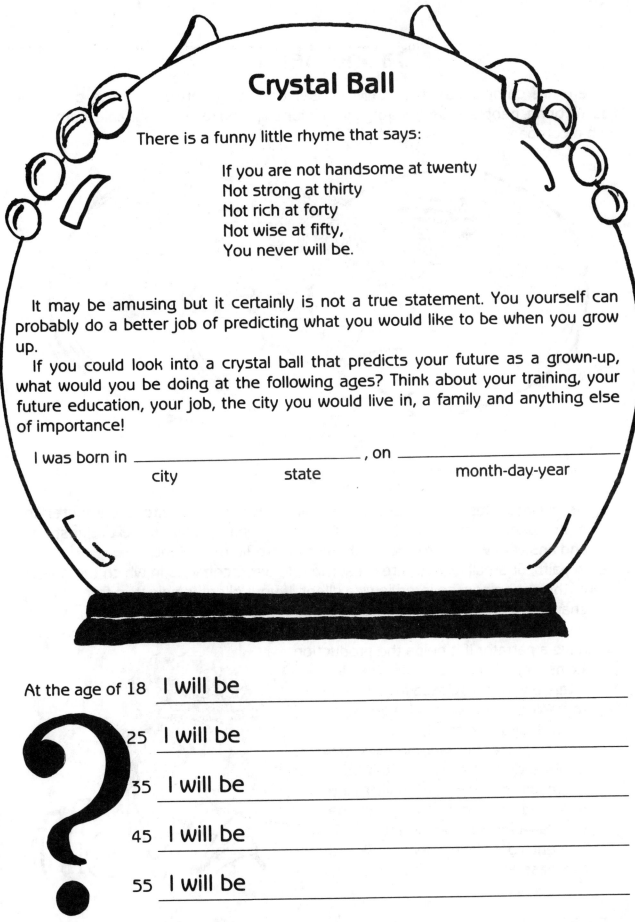

There is a funny little rhyme that says:

If you are not handsome at twenty
Not strong at thirty
Not rich at forty
Not wise at fifty,
You never will be.

It may be amusing but it certainly is not a true statement. You yourself can probably do a better job of predicting what you would like to be when you grow up.

If you could look into a crystal ball that predicts your future as a grown-up, what would you be doing at the following ages? Think about your training, your future education, your job, the city you would live in, a family and anything else of importance!

I was born in _____ , on _____
        city   state   month-day-year

At the age of 18   I will be _____

25   I will be _____

35   I will be _____

45   I will be _____

55   I will be _____

No one can predict the future; however it is always good to hope that you will be the very best you can be!

43

GA1082

Dating Service

There are companies which call themselves dating services whose business it is to bring people together for companionship. Make up a suitable name for such a company.

1. As a class, design a questionnaire which will be fed into a computer to match people according to interests and personality. What kinds of questions and answers would provide a satisfactory profile of a client?

2. In pairs, or small groups, create some role play scenarios in which the owner of the dating service interviews a client. If your client is selected from strong characters in folklore, modern realistic fiction, Mother Goose, or Greek mythology, the interview could be funny and out of the ordinary? You may have a narrator if it helps the production.

3. Consider, for one episode, an interview with Narcissus from Greek mythology who was so egotistical that he spurned the love of everyone because, he said, no one was good enough for him. Instead, he fell madly in love with his own image reflected in a pool of water in the woods—which he never left.*

4. Present your dating service skit to the class.

---

*For more modern day issues for role play based on Greek mythology, see the Good Apple publication *Mighty Myth* by Lipson and Bolkosky, 1982.

Dear Blabby

In almost every newspaper there is a daily syndicated column where people write in for help with personal problems. Though each writer's identity is concealed, unsigned letters will not be accepted. What is the name of the advice column in your newspaper? In the old days these columns were called "Advice to the Lovelorn." However, we now recognize that people have problems dealing with a great range of difficulties which they are reluctant to discuss with folks they know.

It is possible to duplicate this advice column by introducing a "Dear Blabby" mailbox designed to receive mail from people who need help. Keeping in mind the kinds of problems students have, each person will write a letter with a realistic problem in search of an answer. The letter writer will remain anonymous but must use his/her real name only for the teacher's information and also use a fictitious name (a nom de plume) like "Bubbles of Bay City" or "Hapless Harry," for purposes of answering the problem.

The letters that are received will be reviewed by the teacher who will select letters which are of common interest to be read aloud. After each reading a discussion in search of a solution will follow. "I believe that Molly Meek should . . . ." "I don't agree with you. A better thing for Molly Meek to do is . . . ." Is there more than one solution for a problem? How would you classify the problems that writers expressed in their letters to "Dear Blabby" in your classroom?

Solutions may be offered by return mail, if this is preferred. Do not reveal the name of the respondent giving the advice. The activity is open to variations—always taking care to respect students' feelings.

GA1082

Design a Poster

You have contacted a very famous person to talk to students at the next all-school assembly. The celebrity has agreed to make an appearance with the provision that you take care of the necessary publicity. You are anxious to have a big audience and circulate the news all over the school. You have made the necessary decisions about the PLACE, DAY, DATE, TIME, ADMISSION and TOPIC. Remember to include the name of the celebrity (anyone you want).

Design an impressive poster which announces the event. Make it attractive, easy to read, and informative. Don't spare the colors.

MAKE SOME SKETCHES HERE·····

You have designed such a knockout poster that the principal has invited you to travel around the classrooms in school and deliver a one-minute speech about the guest speaker. This speech should include biographical information about the celebrity and give reasons why everyone will want to see and hear your guest. If you can't think of a celebrity you would like to invite, have a brainstorming session and list all the people who are currently popular.

Prepare your one-minute speech and present it with your poster to the class.

GA1082

Detroit Zoo

At the Detroit Zoological Park, one of the most beautiful zoos in the country, there is a sign which many people stop to read with a bemused expression. What is the sign all about? It invites children and adults alike to figure out the collective names of animals.

"Match each phrase with the proper descriptive term for a group."

Now it's your turn to supply informed answers or to do your best guesswork in response to the following list at the Detroit Zoo.

Match Them Up

1. Pheasants		A. Ostentation
2. Leopards		B. Gaggle
3. Foxes		C. Bouquet
4. Rhinos		D. Knot
5. Chickens		E. Troop
6. Heron		F. Route
7. Geese		G. Leap
8. Peacocks		H. Peep
9. Toads		I. Siege
10. Kangaroos		J. Skulk
11. Owls		K. Parliament
12. Wolves		L. Clash

    GA1082

Dialogue: Insights

Think about a book you have read and enjoyed.

The title of the book is   *It's Tough to Be a Kid*

The author is   Malcolm Blain

The character in the book I like best is   Joshua

Some of the things Joshua said were:

(Include at least five statements. Either quote exactly, recall in your own words, or make up some things the character could have said.)
Enclose the quotes inside an *outline picture of the character's face.*

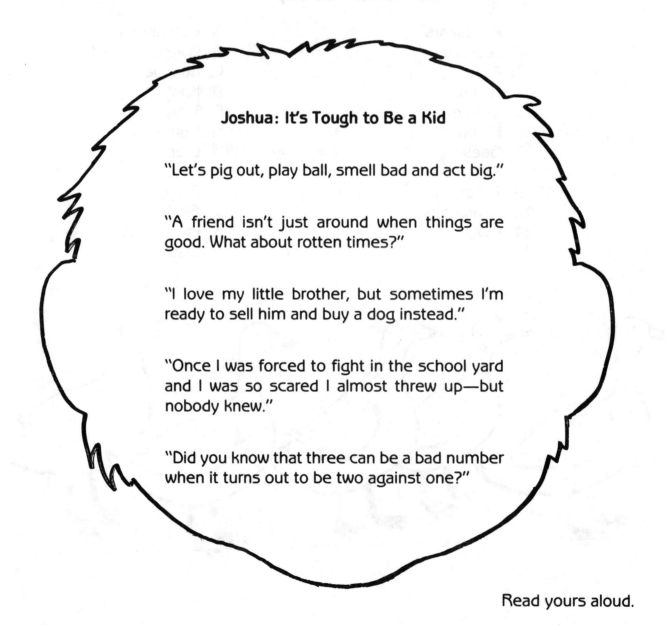

Joshua: It's Tough to Be a Kid

"Let's pig out, play ball, smell bad and act big."

"A friend isn't just around when things are good. What about rotten times?"

"I love my little brother, but sometimes I'm ready to sell him and buy a dog instead."

"Once I was forced to fight in the school yard and I was so scared I almost threw up—but nobody knew."

"Did you know that three can be a bad number when it turns out to be two against one?"

Read yours aloud.

48

GA1082

Diamante: a Diamond Poem

Diamante is the Italian word for diamond. It is also the name for a form of unrhymed poetry invented by Iris Tiedt, who gave it this name because of the physical appearance of the poem on paper. There are two patterns of diamante poetry. Pattern I deals with the same topic from start to finish, while Pattern II deals with opposites and is more challenging.

You will be working from the top of the diamond, going down, with the "topic" and from the bottom of the diamond going up with the "antonym."

The fourth line, in the middle, is tricky, because it is there when the change occurs and the "topic" turns into the "antonym."

Study this diamante poem carefully before proceeding. See how it works from the top, middle and bottom.

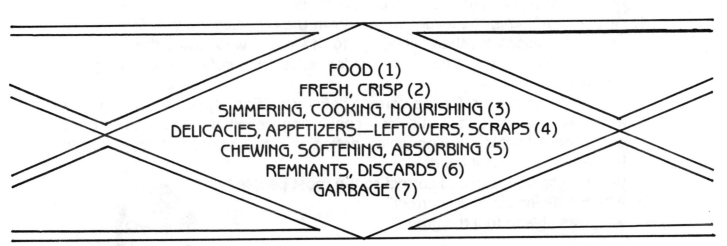

FOOD (1)
FRESH, CRISP (2)
SIMMERING, COOKING, NOURISHING (3)
DELICACIES, APPETIZERS—LEFTOVERS, SCRAPS (4)
CHEWING, SOFTENING, ABSORBING (5)
REMNANTS, DISCARDS (6)
GARBAGE (7)

Directions:
1. Name the topic noun, line 1.
2. Name the antonym (opposite), line 7.
3. Select two describing words for the topic noun, line 2.
4. Select two describing words for the antonym, line 6.
5. Generate three action words for the topic noun (verbs or *ing* words), line 3.
6. Generate three action words for the antonym (verbs or *ing* words), line 5.
7. Decide on two nouns which fit the topic noun, line 4.
8. Decide on two nouns which fit the antonym, line 4.

Suggested topics using opposites:

weak-strong	rich-poor
car-wreck	giant-midget
funny-serious	tortoise-hare
earth-space	day-night

It will help to make a rough copy first. Draw a large diamond on your paper with inside lines.

Greta Lipson and Jane Romatowski. *Calliope: A Handbook of 47 Poetic Forms.* Carthage, Illinois: Good Apple, Inc., 1981.

49

GA1082

Dictionary Game

This game is a great way to encourage dictionary skills while having fun at the same time. This is an activity which is sure to generate brain power and laughs from elementary school to graduate school.

How to play: You will need one dictionary for each group leader and paper and pencil for everyone.

1. Divide into groups or work with the whole class if it isn't too unwieldy. (At any family dinner we play with 10 or 15 members.)
2. The leader of the group looks for a strange sounding word in the dictionary which absolutely no one knows. The leader will pronounce and spell the word correctly to the group.
3. Each group member writes the word on his/her own piece of paper and then makes up a definition which sounds like a genuine dictionary entry. No student names are to be put on the paper.
4. At the same time, the leader writes down the real dictionary definition. The phony definitions are then handed in to the leader who mixes the authentic definition in with the others. The leader reads each definition as the group listens carefully.
5. Now it's time to vote for the correct definition. (Some people may request a second reading of a particularly convincing definition.) The reader goes down the list rapidly asking which definition really sounds correct. A vote is taken by a show of hands.
6. Which definition sounded correct to the most people?
7. Which definition is really correct?
8. Who was able to fool the group?

Some words found by players in our dictionary:

INIAC—The external occipital protuberance of the skull.

OCHRONOSIS—A rare familial disease marked by pigment deposits.

SLOYD—A system of manual training developed from a Swedish system.

OGLALA—A member of the Teton Dakota people, the Oglala.

SPLACKNUCK—The name of an imaginary animal mentioned in *Gulliver's Travels*.

IDGAH—A place set apart for public prayers on the two chief Muslim feasts.

USKOK—A fugitive from Turkish rule of Dalmatian origin.

DROUK—To wet through and through—to soak

Rules:

You can have a good time and forget about points—or

Points may be awarded for fooling others with your phony definitions.

Points may be awarded for guessing correctly.

Points may be awarded for knowing the correct definitions.

Dictionary Revenge*

Have you ever had the experience of asking someone how to spell a word and he says, "Look it up in the dictionary"? Do you get sick and tired of that routine? Doesn't he know that you can't look it up if you can't spell it? If you want to get even, this is your golden opportunity. Invent your own words and put the words in your own dictionary. Call it the _____ Dictionary.

(Your Name)

Now you can tell other people to "look it up."

Example: Snarf: A person who is considered perfect but doesn't care about anyone else.

Word	Definition
1. _____	= The smell of food you cannot stand
2. _____	= The condition of a worm run over by a truck
3. _____	= The sound of fingernails scraped over the chalkboard
4. _____	= The name of a city where everyone has a red nose
5. _____	= The feeling of stepping in mud in your bare feet
6. _____	= The name of someone who drives like a lunatic
7. _____	= A person who eats like a pig does **what** to his food?
8. _____	= An athlete who is conceited and has a big head
9. _____	= The act of fouling things up
10. _____	= An exclamation you shout when your favorite TV program is replaced by a special on rivers and lakes

Remember, you can only use new words which you have invented! Now make up some of your own dictionary entries.

*Thanks to Douglass Campbell and his Creative Problem-Solving Class at Lahser High School, West Bloomfield, Michigan.

GA1082

Diplomacy: Alternatives for Action

Background Story:

Something which resembles a space-ship has landed in a farmer's field near town. A curious nonhuman creature has been observed coming and going from the site. Its activities would indicate that the creature is intelligent. Though it is huge and ferocious looking, there is no evidence that it has done anything wrong or suspicious. What will the citizens decide to do about this intruder? The alternatives for action seem to be that the creature should be (a) investigated (b) exterminated (c) warned to leave (d) welcomed.

List the alternatives on the chalkboard. The students will listen to this dilemma and decide on a course of action as listed. Each of the four corners of the classroom is to represent a different decision and will be clearly marked. The students will take their preferred places depending upon their individual decision.

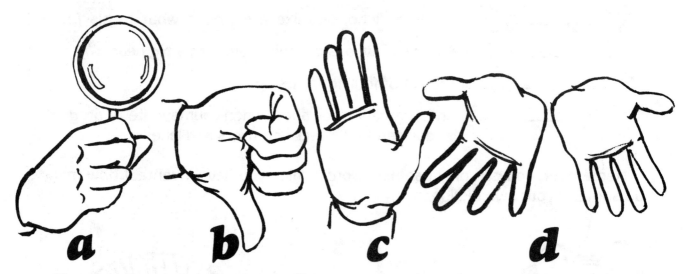

The members of each group will then explain the reasons for their decision to the rest of the class. Everyone is free to express an opinion. If some students are persuaded by the logic of the other groups, they may change groups after everyone is heard. Students will once again discuss their reasons for their change in attitude.*

---

*Greta Lipson and Baxter Morrison. *Fact, Fantasy and Folklore.* Carthage, Illinois: Good Apple, Inc., 1977.

GA1082

Directions: Peanut Butter and Jelly Sandwich

(The teacher must be prepared for this exercise by having a loaf of wrapped sliced bread, a jar of peanut butter, a jar of jelly and a knife.)

One of the most difficult things to do is to give directions to another person or a group so that everything is clear and understandable. Whether we are filling out a form, explaining how a game works, or talking to a class, there will always be a few people who do not understand. We all process and deliver information differently.

The rule to remember is that giving directions requires a step-by-step plan. Never assume that there are some details that people already know. The best demonstration of this is the old "peanut butter and jelly sandwich" routine.* Going counter to our last statement, we expect that most everybody knows how to make a peanut butter and jelly sandwich. It is, therefore, the job of each student to write out *specific* directions for an uninformed reader to follow in order to make the sandwich. (Perhaps someone from outer space!)

The teacher acts the role of the simpleton in this demonstration. Have the unopened ingredients and a knife ready on the desk. After the students' written directions have been handed in, find one that simply says, "Put the peanut butter and jelly on the bread." Like an innocent, the teacher will place the two jars on the wrapped loaf of bread! Pick a few other examples that are equally obscure. Go through the same foolish shenanigans.

The visual message is so strong that the class is now ready to contribute to a *specific* list of directions on the chalkboard.

Ask the students to generalize in other situations. What are the implications of this little exercise? Has anyone ever seen directions for assembling something that said, "Any child can do it!"—but no one at home can figure it out? Why is the phrase "Any child can do it" considered to be such a big joke? How does this apply to much of the gadgetry in your house? What does this tell you about giving and writing "user friendly" directions?

*For this exercise we are indebted to a student teacher and a popular elementary reading series, the name of which is deeply submerged in the past. We hope we may be forgiven this lapse.

GA1082

Endless Sentence: Stretch It

A run-on sentence contains more than one sentence in which somebody forgot to use a punctuation mark in the proper place! But the endless sentence in this activity is madness, with no regard to proper punctuation! The idea here is to start out small and continue to stretch the sentence by adding as many nouns, adjectives, verbs, and adverbs as you can find in your head. Keep it going around the room. Start your motors and begin briefly.

Example:
The car
The yellow car
The flashy yellow car
The flashy yellow car sped
The flashy yellow car sped wildly
The flashy yellow car sped wildly away
The horribly flashy yellow car sped wildly away and streaked crazily
The horribly, nauseating, flashy yellow car sped wildly away and streaked crazily
   with screeching brakes down a . . .

Think: How did the car look?
Think: What did it do?
Think: Where did it go?

   Add mud guards, polka dots, a spare tire, a hood ornament, lace curtains, a tall aerial, a propellor.

GA1082

Epitaphs

An epitaph is a short statement in prose or poetry in memory of someone who has died. Often it is carved into a gravestone which marks the burial place. If one walks through a very old cemetery, one will see a great variety of interesting epitaphs. Most of these are quite serious or quite sweet and loving; others from olden times may be funny or caustic. Epitaphs have a very long history. Two examples from classical literature are

My Own Epitaph
Life is a jest; and all things show it;
I thought so once, but now I know it.
John Gay
(17th century)

Epitaph
Here lies my wife; here let her lie!
Now she's at rest—and so am I.
John Dryden

Epitaphs written as couplets (two liners) or as quatrains (four liners) are most manageable. Here are some examples.

Here lies the Remains of Mr. Joshua Simonds

Departed this Life November 3, 1768

Dear friends for me pray do not weep
I am not dead, but here do sleep

He played his fiddle with zest and joy
'Cause he loved being a country boy!
GBL

Here he lies, good Doctor Platt,
A taste of his medicine knocked him flat.
GBL

Here lies the village baker
He used to bake our pies.
He's happy now in heaven
And baking in the skies.
GBL

Here lies a singer
Who had a sweet throat,
Alas for us all
She's sung her last note.
GBL

Humorous epitaphs can be challenging to compose. Write a funny epitaph for a few of the following: movie star, cowboy, opera singer, clown, animal trainer, mountain climber, race car driver, big game hunter, deep sea diver, doughnut cutter, sky diver, and archaeologist.

Eponyms: You Name It

An "eponym" is a word that is derived from a person's name. It was coined from the Greek words, *epi* (upon) *onyma* (a name). Some of those words are very familiar to us even though we may not know the history of the person responsible for the word. Here are some examples.

1. CANDY   Named for Prince Charles Phillipe de Conde, grandnephew of Louis XIII, King of France (17th century). Charles was a boy with a raging sweet tooth. The court chef, fearful for the absence of nourishing foods in the child's diet, created a sweet glaze to disguise the nourishing foods which he named after Prince Charlie Conde. Everyone went wild for the conde coating (conde coating).

2. LEOTARD   Named for Jules Leotard, a French circus acrobat (1850) who designed a thin, clinging garment that fit like skin and enhanced his form as he performed his aerial somersaults for the delight of his audience.

3. FRISBEE   Named for the Frisbee family, who were bakers in Bridgeport, Connecticut (1930-1940). The company truck drivers would skim Frisbee pie plates across the yard in their spare time. This was known as "plate scaling" and was picked up by students at Yale. Tossing the Frisbee pie plates was later circulated to other schools. The bakery went out of business after WWII, but the Frisbee plates survived and were patented by Fred Morrison in plastic in 1950.

4. LEVIS   Named for Levi Straus, an immigrant from Germany who arrived in California in time for the Gold Rush and designed canvas work pants that wore like iron for miners.

Now it's your turn to name some exciting products after yourself that will go down in the history of marketing. Some suggestions follow:

A dance	Music machine	Automobile
A game	A piece of clothing	Farm machine
A carpenter's gimmick	Food novelty	Library aid
A plumber's helper	A toy	Home appliance

Bonus Assignment:

Be an historian and tell us the fascinating story of how the product named after you came into existence.*

---

*Vernon Pizer. *Take My Word for It.* Dodd, Mead & Co., New York, 1981, pages 14-15.

              GA1082

Ethnic Dishes

In the Good Apple book, *Ethnic Pride*, there is a section which describes foods that were invented by immigrants in America. For example, potato chips were invented in 1853 by George Crum, an American Indian chief. Doughnuts were originally a Dutch "oily cake" but the holes were put in (or taken out) by Hanson Gregory in 1847. The ice-cream cone was invented in 1904 at the St. Louis Exposition by Ernest A. Hamwi and was originally a circular Arabic pastry. Chow mein was created by Chinese laborers working on the Transcontinental Railroad in America in the 1800's. There are many delicious combinations that people have been inspired to concoct.

With a bit of imagination and help from your stomach, you can do it, too! Just think about things like a hot dog on a stick—fried in batter; frozen yogurt; scotch eggs (a hard-boiled egg wrapped in sausage); a one-eyed Egyptian (a slice of bread with a hole in the middle fried with an egg in the center); a banana dipped in chocolate and crushed nuts; round pumpernickel bread scooped out and filled with a spinach and sour cream dip; fruit slush; a banana split.

1. Create a wonderful mouth-watering treat. In a written paragraph describe it well enough so that everyone can appreciate it with you. Give your food creation a name and illustrate it.
2. Describe a favorite dish you love to eat at home. Is it part of an ethnic tradition? Ask at home for the recipe.
3. Collect and reproduce these real and fantasy recipes for everyone. Make a booklet with a cover design using the following poem as the centerpiece.

Win Me with a Regal Charlotte Russe

Wrap me in a grape leaf
Crunch me with chitlins
Tickle me with tortillas
Cool me with vichyssoise
Warm me with Welsh rarebit

Ply me with pita bread
Seduce me with a pizza
Brighten me with beet borscht
Coax me with a curry
Bombard me with baklava

Taunt me with a trifle
Fire me with Szechuan
Pep me with paprikash
Beguile me with weiner schnitzel
Tempt me with sukiyaki

Goad me with gefilte fish
Hound me with haggis
Console me with corn pudding
Josh me with yummy jambalaya

Now soothe me with a sparkling seltzer,
Please!

G. LIPSON

GA1082

Eureka: Invent a Machine

A machine is defined in Webster's Dictionary as "a structure consisting of a framework and various fixed and moving parts, for doing some kind of work." Our vision of work is expanded by the wonders of real and make-believe robots, androids (automatons made to resemble humans) and cyborgs (part human, part machine).

Be an inventor and invent a machine, device, or gizmo that will perform an important function—(a pick-up-the-junk-in-your-room machine). Give your invention a name, illustrate it and label the parts. Write an advertisement that will really create enthusiasm. A radio or TV commercial would be another boost for the sale of your machine! Have a contest for the most outstanding machine devised!

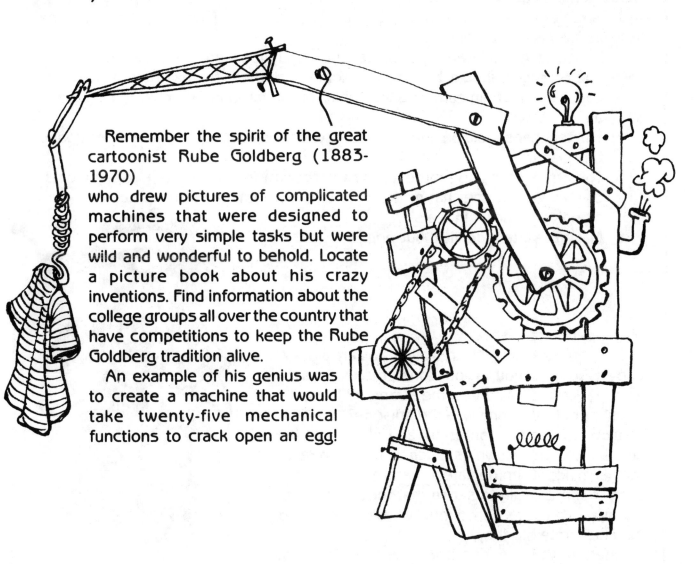

Remember the spirit of the great cartoonist Rube Goldberg (1883-1970) who drew pictures of complicated machines that were designed to perform very simple tasks but were wild and wonderful to behold. Locate a picture book about his crazy inventions. Find information about the college groups all over the country that have competitions to keep the Rube Goldberg tradition alive.

An example of his genius was to create a machine that would take twenty-five mechanical functions to crack open an egg!

Write to: Invent America, U.S. Patent Model Foundation, 1331 Pennsylvania Ave., N.W., Suite #903, Washington, D.C. 20004, 202-737-1836. This foundation offers more than $100,000 in prizes annually for pupils in grades k-8. Children are invited to enter their incentive ideas in a national contest.

GA1082

Eyewitness Reports

It has been demonstrated many times in interviews that eyewitness reports of an event are often conflicting and inaccurate. Eyewitnesses often do not agree about exactly what they see as observers to a scene no matter how casual or dramatic it may be. Because we are not trained to be careful observers, our recall fails us though we may be positive about the details we recollect. This can be demonstrated to the class by making arrangements for a *benign*, unexpected episode which the class will observe. For obvious reasons, never plan on an upsetting or disquieting scenario. Funny and surprising is the very best!

Some suggestions: Think in terms of observable details, in profusion, which students can pick up.

1. Arrange for a stranger to come in and leave at a prearranged time—playing a musical instrument.
2. He walks in and interrupts your teaching as if you were not present.
3. The stranger should be wearing colorful clothes, for example, a baseball cap; a kerchief; an earring; a loud shirt; or the famous Groucho nose, glasses and mustache.
4. The teacher should be quiet but dismayed: "Do you realize you're interrupting this class?"
5. The stranger may be mute, but will execute a few tasks. Walk to the closet; or take out another hat or scarf; or take something from the desk; or grab a book and tuck it into a shirt.
6. Make the interlude vivid but *brief.*

Teacher: Be astonished!

Carry off your part with credibility. You are aghast! Can anybody tell you, in your consternation, exactly what happened? Who was the stranger? Describe the stranger. How long was the episode?

Allow for some confusion and then ask the students to write down as much as they can recall of the incident, immediately, before they forget. Even if some begin to sense that they have been set up, the written accounts will be fascinating. How disparate are they?

When all the papers are in, it is time for class discussion, time to read the papers, and time to emphasize the point of the exercise (aside from fun).

GA1082

Fact or Opinion: Which Is Which?

Everything we read or hear is not necessarily true just because it is printed in a magazine, or newspaper, or reported on a news program. There are different ways of reporting events that can influence the reader to be for or against someone or something. The writer's point of view is something we must be aware of before we make up our own minds. There are certain emotional or "loaded" words that are used which make a very strong impression on us as we read or listen. Verbs (action words); adjectives (describing words); and nouns (names of people, places or things)—all these words do their job well.

Read the paragraph below as an example.

Folk Song Concert

On Saturday, October 10th, twelve hundred howling adolescents shoved their way into Croaker Hall for the annual Folk Song bash. After each of the six wild musical groups performed—the sweaty adolescents broke out into hysterical applause, whistled their brains out, and carried on like a pack of barnyard animals. The food service reports that the young savages swilled down 4000 cans of soft drinks, gobbled up 1500 hot dogs slopped in mustard, and crunched their way through 2000 deafening bags of potato chips. The management considered the pig-out event to be a box-office smash hit.

How does the writer of this article feel about young people and about the folk concert? What words give you the clues about the writer's attitude? Underline the "loaded" words. Rewrite the story just using the basic facts given without revealing any prejudice! It will probably be a very short article. Try this exercise again in a different way. Choose up partners. Each of you write a paragraph which is a straight factual report. Hand your paper to a partner who will use your facts to reveal strong opinions. Remember these opinions can be positive or negative.

GA1082

Fads and Fashions

Since earliest times when humans began to wear animal skins or painted their faces or adorned themselves with necklaces made of animal teeth and claws, fashions have made a statement about life and times. The term *fashion* includes many areas, but this activity will focus on personal fashion which includes clothes, accessories, hair styles, cosmetics and jewelry. This fashion research has four separate activities to choose from.*

A. Describe the fashions which interest you this year.
  1. What do you wear when you want to be casual?

  _____

  _____

  2. What do you like to wear when you want to look dressed up?

  _____

  _____

  3. If you could spend any amount of money for one outfit, what would you buy?

  _____

  _____

  4. Describe the weirdest look you've ever seen.

  _____

  _____

B. Interview your parents, grandparents or older relatives.
  1. What were the fashions when they were preteens or adolescents? List all the items they describe.
  2. Include the approximate dates of the fashions.
  3. A fad is a novelty in fashion that has a sudden burst of popularity and then fades quickly. What were some of the fads your parents remember? What did they consider to be weird when they were young? Exchange notes with the class.

C. Write a description of "Future Fashion in the Year 2050." How do you suppose the population will dress? Will there be any special needs or life-style that will influence fashion?

D. If enough people are interested in pursuing this fashion idea further, the class could hold a dress-up party of the 20's, 60's, or 70's. Hold a class vote—after which everyone will come to school dressed up in the style of that decade.

_____

*Greta Lipson and Jane Romatowski. *Ethnic Pride.* Carthage, Illinois: Good Apple, Inc., 1983.

                                                   GA1082

Fairy Tale Justice

Were Hansel and Gretel a couple of rotten kids who victimized a poor old lady?

The book *Fact, Fantasy and Folklore* features eleven folktales in which the characters are investigated or put on trial in an attempt to arrive at truth and justice. The trial of Hansel and Gretel serves as a prototype for this technique and can be applied to other tales and works of literature as well. The old tale is reread to acquaint the students with the story. In Hansel and Gretel the question is asked: What crimes were committed in this story? Some answers are child neglect, murder, destruction of personal property, stealing.

Hansel and Gretel were apprehended by the police following the oven murder of Mrs. Salem. (But we don't call the old woman a witch just because she was "different" and lived a solitary life in the woods.) The children stand accused of the crime. In an informal hearing there are witnesses (neighbors and relatives) to speak as strong advocates for Hansel and Gretel. Other witnesses (a woodsman and relatives) speak as strong advocates for Mrs. Salem. The entire class listens to the witnesses introduce themselves and hears their points of view. The class then *asks questions* of the witnesses in order to get to the truth and decide who is guilty. Finally, each student writes an independent verdict including the justification for his decision. Who was guilty of a crime in "Hansel and Gretel"?

Choose characters from volunteers and privately orient opposing sides to the issues and attitudes to be expressed. The rest is impromptu. Each witness identifies himself briefly and expresses a point of view, and then responds to class questions. The class is encouraged to ask good, direct questions and not repeat the same ones. After role play of any kind there must always be time for the actors to put aside their characterizations, followed by class discussion of the events, to give meaning and insight to the experience. For similar fairy tale role-play events and specifics, see footnote.

Greta Lipson and Baxter Morrison. *Fact, Fantasy and Folklore*. Carthage, Illinois: Good Apple, Inc., 1977.

GA1082

Family Tree

Make a plan to chart your family tree. The final product may look exactly like a tree or a diagram. An important rule to follow is that the arrangement of people and their relationships should be easy for a reader to understand at a glance. The arrangement should be clear and consistent. For instance, use triangles for male family members and squares for female family members. Talk with your mom and dad, your grandparents, and everyone else who can help you organize the information accurately. Collect information about birth dates (optional) and the maiden (birth) names of the married women in your family. You may start with yourself and then work around your picture or start with grandparents. This can be a small or large production—obviously the size of families varies. Be as fancy and creative as you like. You may discover some surprises as you proceed! Why is this enterprise called a "family tree"?

Follow These Steps

1. Make a list of the names of people you will include. Gather birth dates later (optional).
2. Start with a large piece of butcher paper or something similar, since you may not know how much your tree will spread. Sketch in the arrangement in pencil.
3. The first generation of names will be your grandparents, then your parents, you, brothers and sisters, aunts and uncles (parents' brothers and sisters) and cousins.
4. If you want to use birth dates and your parents do not have exact dates, ask them to estimate the year of a birthday. Use the word *circa* when using these estimates. The word *circa* is a convenient word that means an approximate date: Grandma Bessie Kelly—circa 1925.

Greta Lipson and Jane Romatowski. *Ethnic Pride*. Carthage, Illinois: Good Apple, Inc., 1983.

GA1082

Figures of Speech for Sports

Students will need the sports section of the daily or Sunday paper for this activity.

Sportswriters use powerful descriptive language to capture the excitement of the game. These journalists are known for their colorful verbs and adjectives in describing the action. They don't use ordinary words because it is much more thrilling to read about a team that was *pulverized*; that someone *smashed* a homer; or that a *powerhouse* team *clobbered* the visitors. Sports are packed with action and so the sports section is the most popularly read section of the newspaper by men, women and children.

Collect the sports sections of newspapers and bring them to class for a search for figures of speech in the articles. A figure of speech is defined by Webster as "an expression using words in unusual or nonliteral sense to give beauty or vividness of style; metaphor, simile, personification, hyperbole, etc."

The following phrases are examples:
Tigers whip enemies.
The team performed primitive surgery.
'Gators chew up home team.
Bears put up hairy fight.
Baseball gladiators think Peachtown is the pits.

Activity:
1. Have a Figure of Speech Contest! Divide into teams and see how many figures of speech each group can discover in the sports section of the daily paper.
2. Underline the colorful verbs found in the sports pages, such as *crush, smash, whipped, bolster, roared, slump, fought*. Copy the sentences which include these verbs.
3. Rewrite the sentences substituting the figure of speech with the literal or regular meaning. See how ordinary the sentence is without figures of speech. For example: "They won the game," BOOOORRRRINNNNNG!

For a related activity see Parts of Speech for Sports in the P section.

Greta Lipson and Bernice Greenberg. *Extra! Extra! Read All About It! How to Use the Newspaper in the Classroom.* Carthage, Illinois: Good Apple, Inc., 1981.

Footprint Art

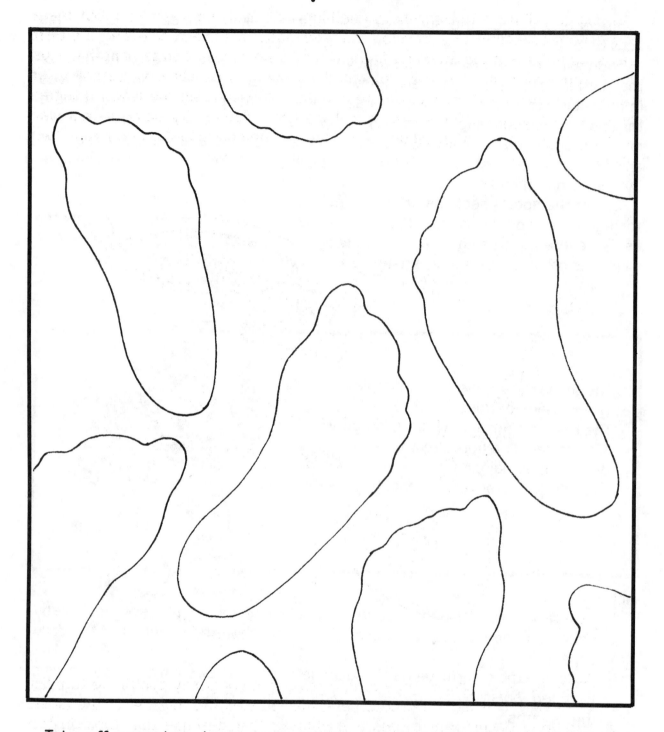

Take off your shoe. Leave your sock on. Place your foot in the middle of a piece of white paper large enough for your entire foot. Stand and trace the outline of your foot with a dark pencil. Now take a good look at the outlined form and create a colorful work of art with your foot as the basis for your artistic endeavor. The foot tracing is uniquely yours and so your illustration should be highly individual. Use your imagination. The picture can be realistic or abstract. Give your drawing a title. Sign your name and date. Display these footprints at your class Foot Fair.

GA1082

Free Form Poetry

It is often difficult to describe something that really interests you. But there is a way of collecting all your good thoughts about a subject, selecting the best ideas, putting them together and finally writing an expressive statement that says it all! You may think that the greatest thing going is baseball or drumming or biking, or movies with popcorn. Here is a way to expand on the lyrical qualities of your favorite topic by writing it in Free Form Poetry. Try doing it this way with the class as the suggestions are listed on the chalkboard and on your own paper.

1. Since everyone must agree on the topic, everyone may contribute to a list of favorite activities. Decide on one that pleases the majority of the class.
2. Everyone brainstorms words and phrases that describe that topic in the most colorful way.
3. As a class, select the strongest and most dramatic words and phrases.
4. Now arrange these words and phrases in the most rhythmic and pleasing order.
5. Write the finished piece with everything in place. Make any final changes that add power and lyricism.
6. Choose someone to read this "free form" class effort expressively.

GA1082

Sample class effort:
   Focus: Baseball
   Ideas generated in brainstorming:

power hitters
all-American sport
strike
grand slam
diamond
triple play
you're out
hometown heroes

the old ball game
hoarse shouting—
      wild cheers
foul ball
sluggers' row
souvenirs
hot dogs, peanuts,
      popcorn

the umpire's blind
kill the umpire
rabid, loyal fans
sunburned
      bleacherites
America's passion
*Doubleday's
      diamond

*(Abner Doubleday invented baseball in 1830, in Cooperstown, New York.)

Final Free Form Poem

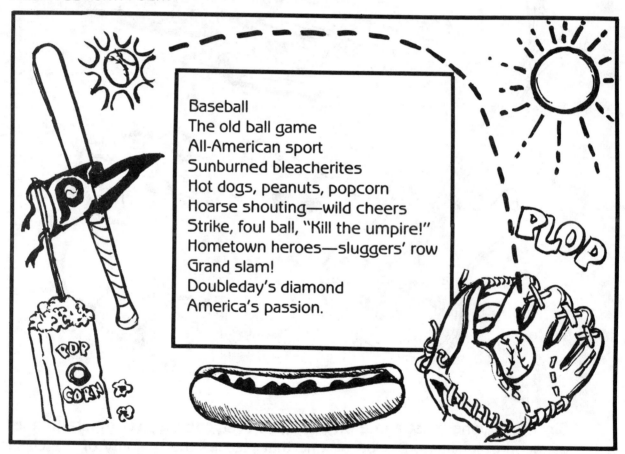

Baseball
The old ball game
All-American sport
Sunburned bleacherites
Hot dogs, peanuts, popcorn
Hoarse shouting—wild cheers
Strike, foul ball, "Kill the umpire!"
Hometown heroes—sluggers' row
Grand slam!
Doubleday's diamond
America's passion.

Read the final product aloud with enthusiasm!

Greta Lipson and Jane Romatowski. *Calliope: A Handbook of 47 Poetic Forms.* Carthage, Illinois, Good Apple, Inc., 1981.

GA1082

Geography Map Game

In the game of Geography each participant may use the name of anything on the map, be it a city, state, town, hamlet, river, ocean, lake, or mountain range. One person starts by naming a place. Others listen for the ending letter of the place name which will be the beginning letter for the next student who takes a turn.

For example:
1. One student starts and says Scranton, which ends with *N*.
2. The next person must start with *N* and says New York, which ends with *K*.
3. The next person says Kalamazoo, which ends with *O*.
4. The next person begins with *O*.

Geography can be played with the entire class, giving each person a turn. In such a large group if a participant misses an answer twice, that person is out. Or there may be two, three, or four teams playing with alternating answers from each team. With team play, if the players miss three turns they are out! The rules are flexible to suit the group. Set reasonable time limits for each participant. No coaching from the sidelines, please.

69

Ghost: the Spelling Spirit

The object of this game is *not to earn points!* The entire class may participate in the order in which they are seated. The first person chooses the first letter which is given orally. The players must always have a word in mind which has a minimum of five letters.

Example:　Eric starts . . . . B
　　　　　Rachel . . . . U
　　　　　Marvin . . . . S

Poor Marvin unwittingly spelled a word and he has just earned 1/3 point. If you earn 3/3 points you are the Ghost and are out of the game. The idea is to keep constructing a word to avoid any points.

Example:　Susie starts . . . . T
　　　　　Mark . . . . E
　　　　　Gerrie . . . . F
　　　　　Chuck . . . . It's Chuck's turn but he doesn't think Gerrie had a real word in mind, so he says "I challenge you!" Gerrie tells him the word she had in mind was *teflon.* Poor Chuck just earned 1/3 point, because he challenged and was given a correct response.

The group starts over again! In summary, the rules are

- Use a word with a minimum of four letters.
- If you end a word you earn 1/3 point.
- If you challenge someone's word and he/she gives you a correct response, you earn 1/3 point.
- If you earn 3/3 points, you're out.

GA1082

Gift: for Holidays or Anytime

The book entitled *It's a Special Day* is a chronology of poems and lessons centered around special event days which are observed throughout the school year. In that selection the poem entitled "The Gift" found its way, persistently, into public and parochial classrooms, scouting groups, Sunday schools and other places where children are taught about loving and caring for others. The poem appeared on bulletin boards at so many different times of the year that it was clear that teachers (in their wisdom) perceived that the poem went beyond Christmas and Hanukkah or any of the holiday times, for which it was originally intended.

A favorite activity is to have students copy the poem, in their best handwriting or printing, decorating it with the ornate enthusiasm of young artists, and put it into a gift box with all the formality and graceful fixings that a gift of love deserves. Here it is—complete with the lesson. It does, in truth, speak to all of us.

The Gift
The most precious gift,
I am told,
Is all the love
The heart can hold.

I give it to you;
You give it to me—
There's enough for the world,
And the gift is free.

Will you take my love—
More precious than gold?
It's the finest gift
That the heart can hold.

Greta B. Lipson

Lesson:

A discussion of values is suggested by the poem. We teach children that the true meaning of giving is to offer that which is a portion of ourselves. One may strike a contrast between material gifts—which may be purchased—and the gift of love, which cannot be bought but is the most enduring of all human offerings.

Greta Lipson. *It's a Special Day.* Carthage, Illinois: Good Apple, Inc., 1978.

GA1082

Grand Old Duke of York: Chant, Clap, March

The "Grand Old Duke of York," from Mother Goose, is a wonderful vehicle for reciting a "round" which is a musical canon sung in unison. Each part is continuously repeated, just like "Row, Row, Row Your Boat." The fun part of the "York" round is that it can be accompanied by clapping, on the beat, and marching around the outer limits of the classroom. Rehearsal on the playground or in the gym can be a treat, too! The rhyme has eight lines and can include four groups of people. The round for each new group starts when the group before you says the word *men*.

The first group starts marching immediately with the first word. As each new group starts to sing, they rise, and they also begin to march. Each group claps in time to the rhythm and repeats the round *four* times. After the fourth and last time the rhyme is sung, each group stops and marches in place until the very last group has finished their fourth round. Pay attention so that the conclusion is absolutely silent and coordinated—and that's a trick.

The interesting part of this round is that all kinds of body language and sound variations can be used to make it quite thrilling—especially when drums, other instruments, or sounds are introduced. All suggestions from students and the music teacher are welcome.

The Grand old Duke of York,
He had ten thousand *men*;

He marched them up to the top of the hill,
And he marched them down again.

And when they were up, they were up,
And when they were down, they were down.

And when they were only half-way up,
They were neither up nor down.

GA1082

Helium Balloon Messages

To demonstrate the wonders of air movement and the objects that float through it, send up your own helium balloon. Helium can be purchased in tanks as seen at state fairs, etc. Look in the Yellow Pages of your telephone book under "Balloons." Find out how far the wind and air currents will carry the helium balloon. Attach your "air mail" message with the date, your name, school address and room number enclosed in protective plastic. Indicate that this is a weather experiment your class is conducting. Ask the finder to please write a note back to you indicating in what city and state the balloon was found. Ask for additional information or comments.

Wait for a day with a vigorous breeze to give the balloon every flight advantage. Launch the balloons from the playground or a safe place *away from trees and traffic*. Once released, the balloons are free spirits. *Do not run after them!*

When the class has received some answers from the "finders," write a human interest story about your weather experiment for a local paper or your class paper including the results, whether startling or disappointing.

Reading some information about weather and how air travels will enhance this balloon launching experience!

Helium Balloon Message— For Fun and Science

Type or write with waterproof ink. Enclose your message in a plastic bag. Tie it securely with string to the neck of your balloon.

Date _____

My Name_____

School_____ Grade____ Room_____

School Address _____

City _____ State_____ Zip_____

Message:

_____

Many Thanks for Your Cooperation on Behalf of Our Class!

Finder's Name _____

Address_____

City _____ State_____ Zip_____

Time Found _____ Date _____

Place Found _____

Return Message:

When you find the balloon, please send your message back to the address above.

GA1082

Heracles' 13th Labor

In the Greek myths Heracles (Hercules) was the strongest man in the world. From the time he was an infant he showed that he had greater strength than other adult men. He was only a year old when he killed two snakes that threatened to strangle him and his infant brother in their crib. He grew to be a powerful athlete who was adored by everyone, but he became arrogant and spoiled. Worse yet, he developed a violent temper and when he couldn't have his way he was forever hurting people as if he were a wild animal! But soon he was punished for his cruel treatment of others. To repent his sins, he went to a priestess at Delphi who sent him to the King of Mycenae. It was this king who gave Heracles twelve gigantic tasks to perform to atone for the evil he had committed. These were called "The Labors of Heracles." It often seemed as if each encounter would kill him!

The task which seemed the easiest for Heracles was his sixth labor in which he was commanded to clean the filthy Augean Stables in twenty-four hours. The three thousand oxen that lived there had been neglected for thirty years and lived in unspeakable filth. Though he was not the brightest of men, Heracles decided to lift two rivers and heave them into the stables. This clever strategy worked and the water rushed through in a tumbling roaring flood and washed everything clean in its path.

If you had to think up a gigantic thirteenth labor for Heracles, what would it be? Remember that he was half-god and had incredible strength. Head your paper "Heracles' 13th Labor." The complete story of Heracles' twelve labors can be found in your library. These are astonishing tales, especially the one in which he agreed to take the world off the shoulders of Atlas and hold it for a while!

Greta Lipson and Sidney Bolkosky. *Mighty Myth: A Modern Interpretation of Greek Myths for the Classroom.* Carthage, Illinois: Good Apple, Inc., 1982.

GA1082

Hinky Pinky: Terse Verse

Hinky pinky, compact language, or terse verse all describe the same language exercise. There are two forms of the hinky pinky.

A Definition Hinky Pinky:
A sneaky insect is a sly fly.
A carpenter is a hammer slammer.
Messy homework is sloppy copy.
   Notice the two-word answer that always rhymes.

A Question/Answer Hinky Pinky:
What did the fish say to the bait? Squirm, worm.
What did the rat say to the trap? Cheese, please.
What do you call someone who studies mummies? A Tut Nut.
   Notice the two-word answer that always rhymes.

SLY FLY

   It may be easier to create hinky pinkys if you work on rhyming words first and then go backwards. In that way you can figure out an appropriate question or a request for a definition. Try to create some of this terse verse with a partner. Take a piece of paper and fold it in half.

What did the fish say to the bait?

Choose your best question and print it on the outside flap. Open up the folded paper and print your answer inside. These can be displayed in the room for everyone to read—but the best part of the folded papers is that there is a blank moment in search of an answer until you lift the flap and discover the clever solution!*

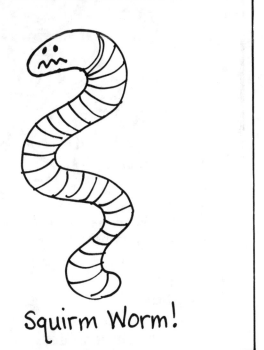

Squirm Worm!

*Greta Lipson and Jane Romatowski. *Calliope: A Handbook of 47 Poetic Forms.* Carthage, Illinois: Good Apple, Inc., 1981.

GA1082

Hokey Headlines

The function of a headline is to summarize the contents of the most important story on the front page. The larger the headline, the more important the story. Some guidelines for writing headlines are

    a. Compress the information. Capture the main idea.

    b. Use the verb in the present tense—(it makes it sound as if the news is happening now).

    c. Use your local newspaper as a punctuation guide to capitalize your headline.

    d. Use humor and imagination.

    e. Use articles *the, a, an* sparingly. Omit other words which are unnecessary.

    f. Don't use weak verbs (action words).

COW OVERSHOOTS MOON

Write your own funny headlines from any source—literature, history, fairy tales, modern times or the future.

For example:

    — Egg Head Goes to Pieces on Wall Street (Mother Goose)

    — Roman War Stops for Caesar Salad (History)

    — Tragedy Shakes Peers of Two Households (Literature—Romeo and Juliet)

    — Pizza King Earns Big Dough

    — Bears Sue Trespassing Blonde

    — Indians Discover Popcorn

    — Cow Overshoots Moon—Lost in Space

    — Homework Machine Newest Rage

    — Laboratory Robots Play Hookey

GA1082

Homophones: Here Hear!

Homophones can cause a lot of trouble! These are words that sound the same but have a different meaning and a different spelling: Mary, merry, marry; pair, pare, pear; pale, pail; mousse, moose. To use homophones correctly, you must use context clues. The sentence tells you which choice to make. Do you eat a stake or a steak? Do the brakes or the breaks stop your car? Do you wear shoes on your feet or feat? With the class, brainstorm as many sets of homophones as you can think of.

Make up a sentence or more which uses the sets of homophones together in a phrase or a sentence which can be illustrated.

1. Mary is feeling merry because she is going to marry her high school sweetheart! Illustrate your statement.
2. I served the moose some chocolate mousse for his dessert.
3. The board was bored with the conversation.
4. Who beat the beet so terribly?
5. Can you believe the horse is hoarse?
6. The queen who reigns my country hates it when it rains.
7. Great, grate
8. Seams, seems
9. Knight, night
10. Feat, feet
11. Not, knot
12. Herd, heard
13. Bare, bear
14. Flour, flower
15. Stair, stare
16. Made, maid
17. Fair, fare
18. New, knew
19. Bow, bough
20. Waist, waste
21. Weather, whether
22. Stake, steak
23. Would, wood
24. Blew, blue
25. Air, heir

If you think you can stand it, write a narrative paragraph in which all the wrong homophones are used!

GA1082

How Old Are You Exactly?

My name is _____

I was born in the year _____

The month was _____

The date was _____

The day of the week was _____
    (make up the day if you don't know)*

I will guess that the time I was born was _____
                    a.m.   p.m.

RIGHT NOW!

This year is _____

This month is _____

This date is _____

This day is _____

This hour: _____ This minute: _____ This second: _____

I am _____ years old
I am _____ months old
I am _____ weeks
I am _____ days
I am _____ hours
I am _____ minutes
I am _____ seconds   OLD!

Remember, there are 12 months in a year, 365 days and 52 weeks. There are 7 days in a week, 24 hours in a day, 60 minutes in an hour, 60 seconds in a minute. Every 4 years there is a leap year which has 366 days and is reflected in an additional day—February 29. How do people celebrate their birthdays when they were born on a leap year?

*For a real treat, find a "perpetual calendar" in an encyclopedia which will give you the day of the week on which you were born for any year up to 2030! It is wonderful to read.

78

Human Knot: Communicate and Cooperate

How important is clear communication? How does it help us solve problems? Obviously people must first communicate, listen, and understand each other in order to cooperate effectively. The Human Knot is an excellent activity to demonstrate these points emphatically.* It is interesting to note that this activity also establishes at least one person who naturally assumes leadership and is responsible for untangling the Human Knot. The teacher works the students into the knot but does not assign a leader nor give directions. Once the knot is developed, the participants are to untangle themselves *without letting go of hands*. Anyone in the knot may give directions. Everyone listens and follows directions to help untangle the crowd. This is a funny and puzzling exercise that establishes a warm sense of community. Since only ten or twelve people participate, the observers may have a chance the next time to solve the tangle but *without using spoken directions*! An untangled knot results in one unbroken line of people. What are the reflections of the students following this exercise?

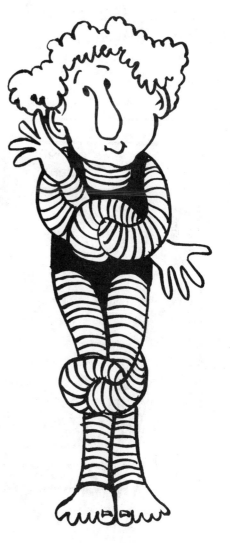

Directions

1. Use an even number of students to participate. Ten or twelve is a good number.
2. All face in one direction in a circle. Each person faces the back of the person in front of him.
3. All put right hand into the center of the circle.
4. Extend the right hand and clasp the right hand of someone standing opposite you.
5. With your left hand, clasp the left hand of someone else who is *not* opposite you.
6. Do not hold both hands of one person!
7. The teacher will choose one person and break one hand free—either the right or left hand. That leaves a human knot of people.
8. Untangle the knot! If done properly, the unknotted group will become a line of people with joined hands.
9. A variation would be to attempt to unknot the crowd *without* the benefit of talking.

*With gratitude and enduring affection, thanks to George Monroe, Principal, Dearborn Schools, for showing us the Human Knot.

 GA1082

Hundred Dollar Word: Spelling

On a piece of paper, assign each letter of the alphabet a place number in dollars. A = \$1, B = \$2, C = \$3, D = \$4, E = \$5, F = \$6, G = \$7, H = \$8, I = \$9, J = \$10. Complete the entire alphabet code in this way. You are in search of a hundred dollar word and must select a spelling word which you think you can decode to add up to that big money. This may be done with several students at the board, solo at their desks, or in teams.

If you choose *pizza* here is what happens.

pizza   p = \$16
            i =   9
            z = 26
            z = 26
            a =   1
                \$78 total

Sorry, good try. Try again. (Is there another strategy you could use to find the \$100 word?)

GA1082

Hyperbole: You Exaggerate!

When you deliberately exaggerate in writing or speaking, because you want to create a strong effect, you are using a figure of speech called hyperbole. You have always heard people using hyperbole and you have always used it yourself! It must sound familiar to you when you hear "I am so hungry I could eat a horse." (Really?) "I've told you a million times to sit down." (That's not true!)

Can you think of others you have heard around school or home? Below, you will find twelve questions to which the answers could be written using hyperboles. Answer in complete statements. Add some remarks you have heard which use exaggeration for effect.

1. How high was the birthday cake?
2. How strong was the truck driver?
3. How many dishes did he leave in the sink?
4. How sick did the roller coaster make the kids?
5. How fast is the car?
6. How mad was his father?
7. How dirty was the baby?
8. How much did you laugh at the comedian?
9. How loud was the rock group?
10. How hard are you working?
11. How happy will you be on the last day of school?
12. How hot was it?

1. Compare your hyperboles with others in your class. Can you use this same kind of list for different hyperboles?
2. Can you think of more original hyperboles than "I am so hungry I could eat a horse"? Could you eat a hippopotamus? A gorilla? An elephant? Try it with the whole class and use your imagination.

Idioms

Idioms are common expressions which we all use, and we all understand (more or less), but when translated literally they don't make a whole lot of sense! When you say, "I'm up a tree!" it doesn't have anything to do with your position in a tree. Instead it means that you have reached an impasse; that you are in a bad spot with no place to go; you're stumped, (pun) or puzzled, or you have no solution to a problem.

Because idioms are so much a part of our informal language and are figurative expressions, they are very difficult for the nonnative English speaker to understand. Idiomatic expressions are unique to geographical regions and areas. Northern and Southern United States' idioms are different from each other as are those found in Western and Eastern United States.

When we say to someone, "Go jump in the lake," we mean "Take a walk," which means "Buzz off," which means "Beat it," which means "Get out of my face," which means "Get lost," which means "I'm fed up with you," which means "Go peddle your fish," which means "You're buggin' me," which means "Don't push your luck" . . . ! Is language great or is it great?

Another problem with idioms is not only that they are regional and ethnic, but they are forever changing, are faddish and may be incomprehensible to many people after a few years. Ask someone old enough to be your great grandparent to explain "23 Skidoo." But if certain idioms hang around long enough, some of them may become proverbs—"It isn't whether you win or lose, it's the way you play the game" or "A miss is as good as a mile."

We all use idioms in our speech every day of our lives, but we are generally not aware of them. Consider the following idioms. What do they mean? Start an idiom collection and every time you hear one, write it down on a specially prepared *Idiom Graffiti Post* in class. Listen to your teachers' idiomatic expressions as well.

Idiom Samples

1. He has a chip on his shoulder.
2. Turn over a new leaf.
3. A fine kettle of fish.
4. He's off his rocker.
5. You took the words right out of my mouth.
6. Head honcho.
7. Like it or lump it.
8. A pain in the neck.
9. What a bummer.
10. Bag it.
11. Let it all hang out.
12. Cool it.
13. Flipped her lid.
14. Blew his stack.
15. Read the riot act.
16. Don't wear your heart on your sleeve.
17. It caught my eye.
18. This is a vicious circle, a wild goose chase.
19. I'm walking on eggs.
20. It's the straw that broke the camel's back.

GA1082

Incredible Edibles

You are going to name a candy bar using your own first or last name! Brainstorm the names of all the candy bars you can think of to be written on the chalkboard. Decide on a brand name using your first or last name or both your names. Having thought up this "new" candy bar, design an attractive, colorful wrapper. List on the wrapper all of the good qualities which describe you as if they were the ingredients. For example, here are some candy bars developed by other students.

"Good 'N Jenny"   "Bilky Way"   "Barbara Ruth"

"Milky Wayne"   "Jay Day"   "Powell House"

"Milk Doug"   "Kim Kat"   "Jim Bo Block"

"Ahmed Joy"   "Chris Crunch"

"Carrie Mel"   "Marv-Cateer"

Good 'N Jenny

Ingredients:
Black hair, brown eyes, generous, smart, cheerful, good sport, Puerto Rican, helpful . . . (include at least 10 positive qualities)

If you have a great idea for any other product to use with your name, then go ahead with the same plan.

GA1082

Index Cards: Spatial Construction

Believe it or not—index cards can be used for something other than taking notes and filing! This project takes cooperation, steady hands, patience, and imagination. You must not move too suddenly or exhale too heavily.

The first steps require an orderly approach. Count off by fours to organize your groups. From a designated place at the back of the room, collect sixteen or more index cards and a bundle of paper clips (keep count of the additional number of cards used). On a solid surface begin to construct something that can only be built with the use of the cards and paper clips. Sometimes the creation begins to change along the way. You may bend the cards, shape them in any way, or use in any position. After careful and thoughtful construction, be prepared to present the construction to the class. Explain what it is, what purpose it serves, and give it a name. Include details of any problems and solutions encountered along the way.

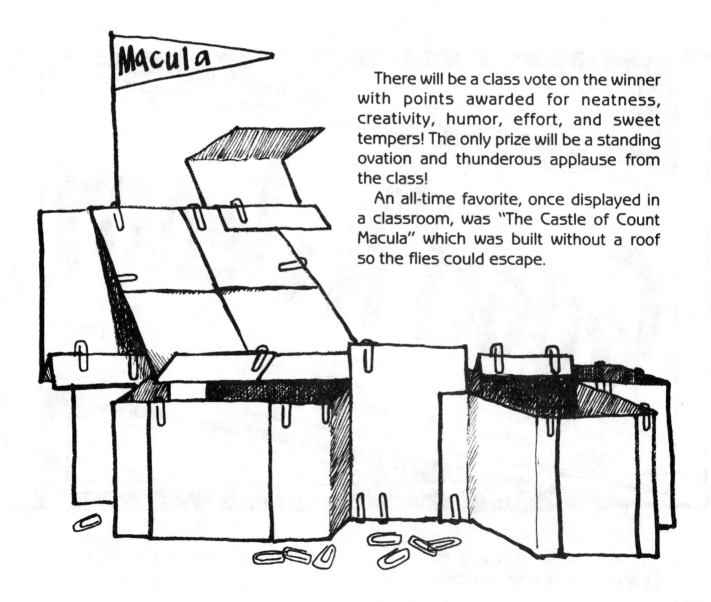

There will be a class vote on the winner with points awarded for neatness, creativity, humor, effort, and sweet tempers! The only prize will be a standing ovation and thunderous applause from the class!

An all-time favorite, once displayed in a classroom, was "The Castle of Count Macula" which was built without a roof so the flies could escape.

GA1082

Initialisms: FYI

In books, movies, TV, newspapers, radio and in everyday life, we are accustomed to reading and hearing initials being used instead of names. These initials stand for businesses, organizations, agencies and even people. There are so many references of this kind that we could almost read an entire paragraph full of these initials and know what they mean. It might look something like this:

My teacher, who belongs to the NEA, went on a TWA flight to NYC. He was looking forward to an IRA meeting there and planned to visit his sister, too. She belonged to NOW and was coming in from L.A. in a GM car to promote action on the ERA. Crowds filled the airport on their way to the G.O.P. convention. Some big heroes from the NFL were on the same flight as my teacher. There were also some VIP's from the UN who were being taken around by some C.E.O.'s from IBM. When the FBI showed up at the gate, everybody knew there was trouble brewing. A business-like agent handed my teacher a note which had F.Y.I. written on it! The messenger said to him, "We need your answer A.S.A.P.!"

Brainstorm another list of initials and write your own tricky paragraph.

NEA	National Education Association
TWA	Trans World Airlines
NYC	New York City
IRA	International Reading Association
NOW	National Organization for Women
L.A.	Los Angeles
GM	General Motors
ERA	Equal Rights Amendment (to the Constitution)
G.O.P.	Grand Old Party—Republicans
NFL	National Football League
VIP's	Very Important Persons
UN	United Nations
C.E.O.'s	Chief Executive Officers
IBM	International Business Machines
FBI	Federal Bureau of Investigation
F.Y.I.	For your information
A.S.A.P.	As soon as possible
T.G.I.F.	Thank goodness it's Friday
C.A.P.P.	Child Assault Prevention Program

The sports section of your paper is full of initialisms. Look and see.

Introduction to Law

Here is a discussion activity that is a real eye-opener for students of all ages. It is from a book entitled *Everyday Law for Young Citizens.** We rarely think about how pervasive and important the function of law is in every aspect of our lives. If it is true that the law affects everything—try to prove that statement. When do we have our first encounter with the law and in what ways?

Hints for Discussion on How the Law Influences Our Lives from Cradle to Grave

You may think of the sequence of events from the day of your birth to the day you come home from the hospital. There are legal processes and documents all along the way: A baby is delivered in a licensed hospital by licensed doctors and nurses with college degrees. The infant is registered on a legal birth certificate and is a legal citizen of the U.S.A. Mother and child are driven home by a licensed driver who must obey traffic laws. Baby is welcomed home by the licensed family dog who bounds out of the family home or apartment which is mortgaged or rented under a legal contract known as a lease. Baby is cuddled by a brother who goes to the neighborhood school because the law requires attendance. Older sister may run an errand for the new family member on her licensed bike, which she rides to the local drug store which is licensed to dispense medicine. The pharmacist who fills the prescription is registered by law . . . . The list never really ends.

Picture yourself as a newly born baby, in the center of a diagram, with a web of people and events surrounding your arrival.

Celebrate *Law Day on May 1st*. For information on programs, materials, services and law-related education in your state, write to: National Institute for Citizen Education in the Law, 605 G. Street N.W., Washington, D.C. 20001, 202-624-8217.

---

*Greta Lipson and Eric Lipson. *Everyday Law for Young Citizens.* Carthage, Illinois: Good Apple, Inc., 1988.

GA1082

Keep a Log: the Week in Review

Introduce the students to the idea of keeping a personal log in which they will write entries on Friday to sum up their week. A stenographer's notebook is easy to handle—but any bound notebook will do.

After a week of schoolwork and activity, the student can reflect upon what has happened, reflect on good times and bad—and sort through impressions of that particular five-day block of time. Though the log is personal, some students may want to share their logs with the teacher and that is acceptable. The teacher need only comment in a log with a single responsive or supportive sentence: "I'm happy for you"—"We've all had days like that"—"I knew you could do it"—"I know how you feel"—"You did your best"—"Stay with it"—"I'm proud of you."

Sometimes students feel that they have absolutely nothing to write! If that is the case, they could write that down. Describing the blankness of a Friday after-noon, the tiredness, the pleasure of looking forward to the weekend may be the beginning or the sum total of a student's statement for the week. The statement "I have nothing to say about anything because it's been a dumb week" is adequate and oftentimes it acts as a catalyst.

The objective of the log is to contemplate events and express oneself in writing. Not only does this help define the world around us but the very act helps refine the art of writing purposefully. It should be added that reading a student's log should be an opportunity to share rather than to be intrusive. Be sensitive to community feelings in this regard.

Letters into Words: Contest

Organize two teams and give each team a name with personality like the Chargers or the Cadillacs or the Dukes. The point of this competition is that each team will be assigned one letter from which they may think of as many words as they can that begin with the letter. There is a sixty-second time period for each team. Each word called out earns a point. Write the team names on the chalkboard to record points.

Start by giving the Dukes one letter from the following group: *s c p a b m t d r h*. Any team member may then call out a word starting with the assigned letter. In the sixty-second segment all team members can call out words as often as they are able. There are to be no repeats or variations of any words (jump, jumped, jumping). Keep a close tally of the points for the Dukes in the sixty-second time segment. Now it's the Chargers' turn with a different letter from the same group of letters. Start a tally on the board for them.

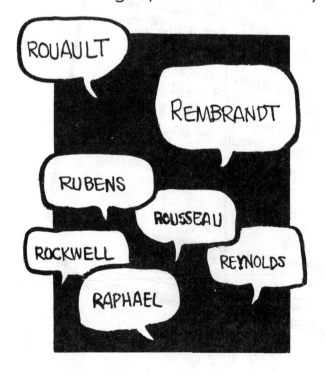

As students become more practiced with the game, they may want to work with letters that produce a lower frequency of words such as *f e l i g w n o u v k j q y z x*. To make the contest more challenging, the students may want to narrow down choices by choosing words in a particular category such as math, politics, science, books, authors, sports, history or any choice that has appeal.

Student observers can participate at their seats with pencil and paper. They may be able to beat the team efforts even though writing is more time-consuming.

88

GA1082

Lipogram: Word Substitution

Imagine how difficult it would be to write a paragraph or verse without using certain vowels or consonants! This idea is called a lipogram, which is a piece of writing which only has words that do not contain a certain letter. You can make a lipogram with any piece of writing by deciding which letter will be off limits. It can be a very funny exercise using Mother Goose rhymes. Try to re-write the following rhyme by eliminating all words that contain the letter *h.* Substitute a synonym or a reasonable word for the one you cannot use. How does the rhyme read when you are finished? Compare your version with other students.

(Eliminate *H*)

Mary Had a Little Lamb

Mary had a little lamb,
Its fleece was white as snow;
And everywhere that Mary went
The lamb was sure to go.

***

It followed her to school one day,
It was against the rule,
It made the children laugh and play
To see a lamb at school.

***

And so the teacher turned him out,
But still he lingered near,
And waited patiently about
Till Mary did appear.

***

And then he ran to her, and laid
His head upon her arm,
As if he said, "I'm not afraid,
You'll shield me from all harm."

***

"What makes the lamb love Mary so?"
The eager children cry.
"Why, Mary loves the lamb, you know,"
The teacher did reply.

(Eliminate *O*)

Jack Sprat

Jack Sprat could eat no fat,
His wife could eat no lean;
And so, betwixt them both, you see
They licked the platter clean.

GA1082

Literal Word Pictures: Time Flies

There are many expressions we use daily in the English language that we understand quite clearly. However, many of these terms would be quite ridiculous if we gave them a literal translation and drew pictures of the objects suggested by the words. Draw a literal picture of each of the following:

Time flies	A skyscraper	Boxer shorts
A cowboy	A baby-sitter	An egg timer
A football	Eyeglasses	A punch bowl
A watchdog	A swimming suit	A firecracker
A rock concert	A headlight	Raining cats and dogs
A shoe tree	An eggplant	A hot dog to go

Now it's your turn. What expressions can you think of that would translate into very strange pictures?

Love, Live, Five, Jive: Word Exchange

Look at the title. Is there something going on in the choice of the four words, "Love, Live, Five, Jive"? If you haven't already guessed, we started out with the word *love*—changed one letter in the word and it became *live*—changed one letter and it became *five*—changed one letter and it became *jive*.

For the most possibilities in this game, use a word that has four letters; change one letter at a time and turn it into another word each time. The biggest challenge, however, is to write a sentence with each new word italicized and try to make a fairly sensible story by connecting those sentences. Try words such as *sold, sale, lend, heat, bump.*

For example: Start with *land.*

1. I was on the farmer's *land*
2. walking across the steaming *sand*
3. when I found a hideous *hand*
4. wrapped in an old black *band.*
5. It was desperately clutching a *wand*
6. that bent to and fro in the hot *wind.*
7. But I couldn't *find*
8. the *kind* of person
9. with such a twisted *mind*
10. to perform such a stunt in a *bind.*

GA1082

Macaronics: Mix Two Languages

This is an activity for the whole class. *Macaronics* is another word for a coded spoken language called pig Latin. You could use this language if you wanted to communicate a message to another person and did not want others to know what you were saying. You may learn to use pig Latin rapidly, but the listener must also be a fast translator as well—otherwise you will not be communicating.

Pig Latin

Directions:
1. Think of a word. DOG
2. Take the first consonant off the word. That leaves OG.
3. Say OG and finish the word by using the detached consonant with the ending AY. Say OG-DAY (which means "dog" in pig Latin).
4. Try this strategy with other words for practice. (You may write it down.)
   dumb (umb-day)   mother (other-may)   smart (mart-say)
   rich (ich-ray)   fun (un-fay)   silly (illy-say)
5. The system will not work with all the words. When that happens use the correct word.
6. Now try it with a sentence. For example:

"An-cay ou-yay ay-say ome-say ords-way in ig-pay atin-lay or-fay the eacher-tay?" Translated the sentence is "Can you say some words in pig Latin for the teacher?"

Practice first by writing down the complete sentence or phrase you want to translate into pig Latin and work on it word by word. Everyone may not agree on some of the word forms you use, but the rules are not hard and fast. Watch as the words are written on the chalkboard while everyone contributes to the translations.

GA1082

Malapropisms: Sounds Right, Fits Wrong

In 1775 Richard Sheridan wrote *The Rivals* which became enormously popular. One of the reasons for its success was a character Sheridan created whose name was Mrs. Malaprop. Her problem was that she misused words constantly. She would use a word that *sounded* almost like the correct word but really meant something else. "All men are Bavarians" she would intone—meaning that all men were barbarians. The effect was very funny and the audiences loved it. As a matter of fact, the malapropism has survived to the present day because it is such a surefire way to make people laugh. Modern comedians will deliberately do what Mrs. Malaprop did because of its effect on the listeners. Here are a few malapropisms.

The *polo* bears live in the zoo. (polar)
Neon stockings fit very well. (nylon)
I *gargoyle* with mouthwash every day. (gargle)
Are you trying to *incinerate* that I am insincere? (insinuate)
Carry your books in a *totem* bag. (tote bag)

Can you correct the malapropisms above? Now you think of some and use them in sentences! It's not easy.

"POLO" BEARS?

GA1082

Map Making: from Home to School

Can you remember your daily route to school well enough to draw a map? The strange thing about walking the same route every day is that you really may not have noticed everything there is to see! If you have ever wondered about some people who can give exact directions about traffic lights, blocks, and stop signs on the way to a destination, this is your chance to test your skill and memory. Try to be as accurate as you can so that someone could actually locate your house if he/she had never been there before. Remember to indicate north, south, east, west. How many street names can you remember? What cross streets intersect your block? Are there any landmarks you can point out to help someone find the way? Take your finished map with you on your trip home today to double check for details. Are you surprised at how much you knew or didn't know about that familiar trip? Make corrections or additions. Use some symbols or pictures for additional information. Trade your map with a partner who has never visited your home. What additional information does this person need and what other details do you need to have on your partner's map?

Make some observations about maps at the shopping mall that say "You are here." What color-coded legends or devices are used to help you find your way? Are the maps clear or confusing? Describe the problems or excellent features of the maps.

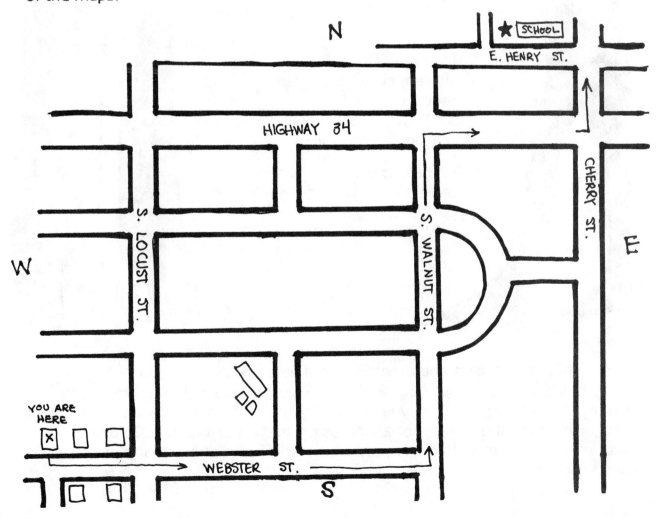

Memory Associations

A proven way to remember groups and categories or series of facts is to make a funny, memorable phrase or sentence from the information. We are more inclined to remember nonsense just because it *is* ridiculous. Here is the technique. Identify the first letter of each word to be remembered. Make a word, sentence, or phrase from these letters.

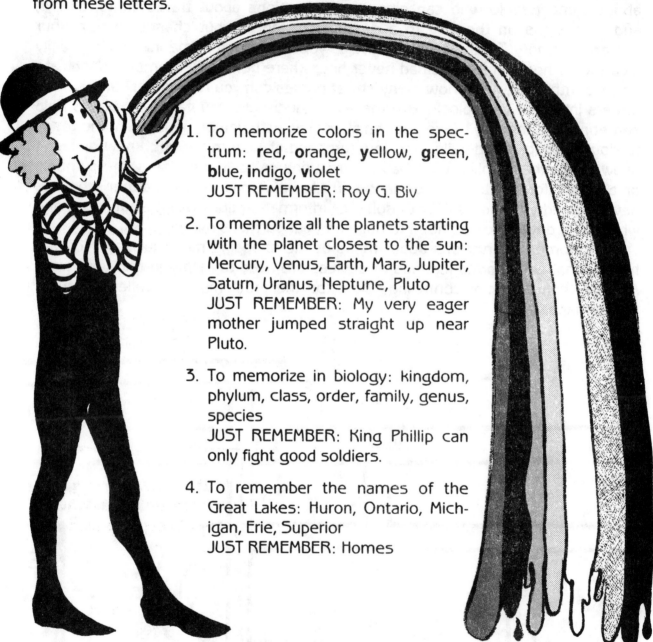

1. To memorize colors in the spectrum: **r**ed, **o**range, **y**ellow, **g**reen, **b**lue, **i**ndigo, **v**iolet
   JUST REMEMBER: Roy G. Biv

2. To memorize all the planets starting with the planet closest to the sun: Mercury, Venus, Earth, Mars, Jupiter, Saturn, Uranus, Neptune, Pluto
   JUST REMEMBER: My very eager mother jumped straight up near Pluto.

3. To memorize in biology: kingdom, phylum, class, order, family, genus, species
   JUST REMEMBER: King Phillip can only fight good soldiers.

4. To remember the names of the Great Lakes: Huron, Ontario, Michigan, Erie, Superior
   JUST REMEMBER: Homes

You may have heard about some of these associations before, or you may have heard different ones. But as long as you realize how it's done, you can make it work for you when you need help to memorize. Make up several of your own weird memory associations using the pattern above. Compare notes with your classmates. Who has produced some associations that can be put to good use?

GA1082

Metaphors

"Juliet is the sun." William Shakespeare.

A metaphor is a figure of speech which *suggests* a similarity between two things which are not alike. This technique creates a strong and colorful statement.
(Do not use the words *like, as, than, similar to, resembles*. When such words are used to strike a comparison, the result is a figure of speech called simile.)

Metaphors:
1. The cloud is a white marshmallow. (They are both white, puffy and soft looking.)
2. The road snakes around the mountain. (They both bend and curve in a serpentine way.)
3. Elevators are roller coasters in my stomach. (They both go up and down dramatically.)

****

Pass out this list for whole class participation or write the following words on the chalkboard. Ask the students to respond quickly by converting each word into a metaphor. "Kisses are candy," "Hate is slow poison," "Sleep is a blanket," "Jealousy is a hidden serpent."

sleep	hate	dreams
night	jealousy	personality
friendship	sunshine	books
parents	fall	vacation
loneliness	winter	kisses
conversation	school	junk food
laughter	anger	science
spring	tears	math

Important!
Keep track of these works of art for the activity on the next page, Metaphor Poems.

GA1082

Metaphor Poems

This activity follows the previous experience with metaphors. (See Metaphors on the preceding page.) Organize groups of four people or work with the students in rows. Each group starts with a metaphor that was developed by the students in the whole class activity. The group should select a line which they think has the best creative possibilities. Write down the line and compose four more lines of poetry to follow. These lines must make sense. These five-line metaphor poems *will not rhyme* but will have a pleasing lyrical flow.

This will be a timed competition. How fast can you produce a poem? Select a timekeeper who will record the time at which the finished groups raise their hands. Who will come in first, second, or third? Regardless of time, which group produced the best metaphor poem?

Laughter is champagne
It bubbles up
Tickles your funny bone
Pops your cork
Goes right to your head

KISS • KISS • KISS

Kisses are candy
A sweet present
Wrapped with care
Lots of flavors
Yummy and delicious

96

Momus the Critic: Mythology

In ancient mythology there is a story of three very spoiled and bored gods who lived in luxury on Mt. Olympus. Because they were always in search of fun and were very competitive, they decided to have a contest to liven things up a bit. Neptune, the god of the sea, Minerva, the goddess of wisdom, and Jupiter, the head god, had an argument over who could create the most perfect thing in existence. They committed themselves to this competition and selected Momus, another god, to be the judge of who had made the most amazing object. This, however, was a terrible mistake since Momus was a well-known fault finder.

The day came for the judging and Neptune unveiled a dazzling white bull that weighed 1500 pounds. This was the first bull ever to exist. Momus said, "This bull's horns are in the wrong place. The horns belong under his eyes so he can see who he is attacking."

It was Minerva's turn and she proudly showed the magnificent house she had built (the first ever to exist). But Momus said, "This house needs wheels so it can be moved away from troublesome neighbors."

Finally, Jupiter showed his wondrous creation which was a person (the first ever to exist). Momus chuckled and sneered, "This person needs a window in its chest! How else can we know its innermost feelings and thoughts without an opening for us to see through!" Nobody won the contest and all three gods were furious with Momus.*

****

What is your reaction to all of this? Write a letter which is critical or complimentary to Momus. Is he a fool or a brain? Think through what you want to say and begin:

Dear Mo,

Sincerely,

---

*Greta Lipson. *Famous Fables for Little Troupers*. Carthage, Illinois: Good Apple, Inc., 1982.

GA1082

Movie Marquee

It would help to have the movie section of the local newspaper for this activity. On the chalkboard, or on your paper at your desk, list movie titles currently showing at neighborhood movie theaters. You may also include some old time movie classics you have heard about or seen on TV. Select ten or fifteen of all the titles listed on the board and write these at the top of your paper for easy reference. The collection of titles will suggest a plot for a story depending upon the flavor and mood of the selections. Underline the titles. The story must make sense and hang together though it can be from the realm of fantasy. Here are some old movie titles.

- *Stand by Me*
- *Radio Days*
- *One-Eyed Jack*
- *Star Trek*
- *Dead of Night*
- *Jaws*
- *Ruthless People*
- *Morning After*
- *The Creature from the Black Lagoon*
- *The Wizard of Oz*

- *Around the World in 80 Days*
- *Animal Crackers*
- *The Little Shop of Horrors*
- *Modern Times*
- *The Pink Panther*
- *The Big Chill*
- *The Long Voyage Home*
- *Mutiny on the Bounty*
- *Ship of Fools*

It was in the <u>Dead of Night</u> that I met <u>One-Eyed Jack</u>. We were both looking into the window of <u>The Little Shop of Horrors</u> and I could tell he wanted to <u>Stand by Me</u>. There were all kinds of strange pastries in the window like <u>Animal Crackers</u>, eclairs shaped like swans and <u>Jaws</u> made out of gingerbread. All at once I felt <u>The Big Chill</u> and it was as if a spell had been cast by <u>The Wizard of Oz</u>. I was transported to the deck of the <u>Ship of Fools</u> with a boat load of <u>Ruthless People</u>. The captain said we would be traveling <u>Around the World in 80 Days</u> before we could make <u>The Long Voyage Home</u>. But there was a <u>Mutiny on the Bounty</u> and the <u>Morning After</u>. . .

GA1082

Mystery Book Clue-In

Motivating children to read some of the finest selections in literature can be accomplished through developing a clue game from books that are read. In one of the most quoted pieces of research (*Anderson, et al., 1985), it has been recommended that students from grades three and above experience a minimum of two hours of independent reading each week. The following activities will provide students with the opportunity to play with information in the form of clues taken from their recreational reading.

Students are provided with a wide variety of trade books through the classroom and school or public libraries. Once they have been given the opportunity to read some of the selections, they are invited to play Mystery Book Clue-In.

The caption "Mystery Book Clue-In" is displayed at the top of a classroom bulletin board. Each day of the week a clue from a mystery book is placed on the Clue-In bulletin board. By the fifth day a list of five clues is displayed. Students are invited to guess the title by writing their answers on slips of paper and placing them in the Mystery Book Box. Answers are tabulated by the teacher or student monitor. Students can make one guess each day after a new clue is added. On the fifth day, after students have had the opportunity to respond to the last clue, the correct title is announced. The student who correctly identified the title the most number of times is declared the winner. There may be a number of winners each week.

---

*R.C. Anderson, E.H. Hiebert, J.A. Scott and I.A.G. Wilkinson. (1985) *Becoming a Nation of Readers: The Report of Commission on Reading*. Washington, D.C.: The National Institute of Education.

GA1082

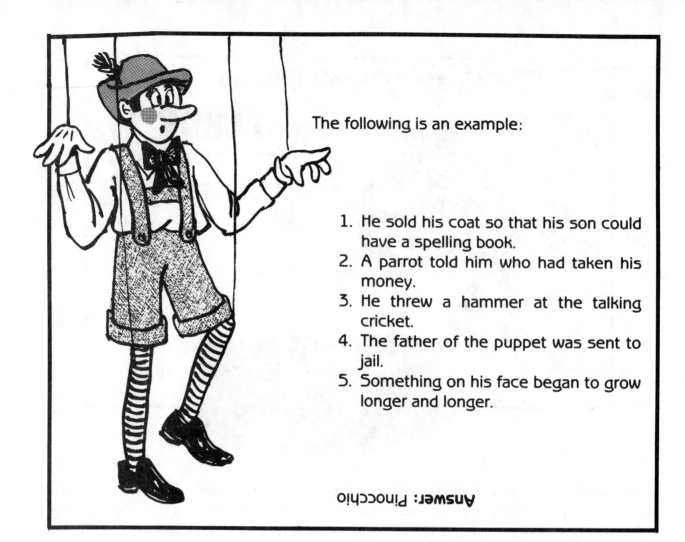

The following is an example:

1. He sold his coat so that his son could have a spelling book.
2. A parrot told him who had taken his money.
3. He threw a hammer at the talking cricket.
4. The father of the puppet was sent to jail.
5. Something on his face began to grow longer and longer.

Answer: Pinocchio

Clue Me In

Clue Me In is a program designed to motivate students from kindergarten through grade seven to read selections which include books by award-winning authors such as Beverly Cleary, Robert McCloskey, Betsy Byars and William Steig. Clue Me In could be compared with television game shows having teams, an electronic response system, an exciting format and the thrill of scoring points. The program which is written for the classroom involves clues referring to specific titles and book characters. For more information, write the Wit Lit Company, 713 Shoreham, Grosse Pointe Woods, MI 48236.*

---

*Reprinted by permission of the publisher, Wit Lit Company.

Name Acrostic: Adjectives

Make a name acrostic which celebrates the wonderfulness of you. Don't be modest and do be creative! Look hard at the letters of your name and spread your good qualities in all directions. Use your first and last names. Think adjectives!

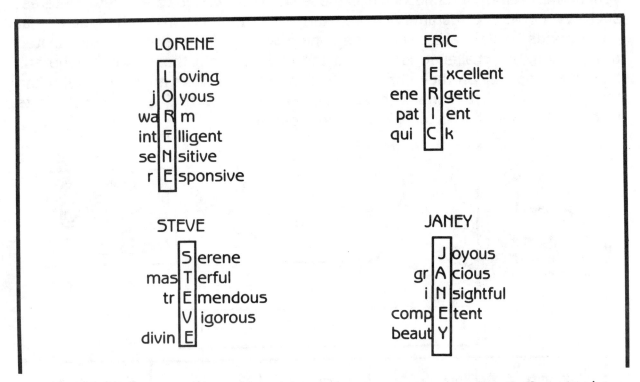

LORENE
- **L** oving
- j **O** yous
- wa **R** m
- int **E** lligent
- se **N** sitive
- r **E** sponsive

ERIC
- **E** xcellent
- ene **R** getic
- pat **I** ent
- qui **C** k

STEVE
- **S** erene
- mas **T** erful
- tr **E** mendous
- **V** igorous
- divin **E**

JANEY
- **J** oyous
- gr **A** cious
- i **N** sightful
- comp **E** tent
- beaut **Y**

After working on your own name, consider making a name acrostic for members of your family, for a good friend, or for your pet. Enclose the total work in a designed crest with ornate borders. Use strong colors and decorative details on your emblem.

Band **J** ock
I ngenious
handso **M** e
A rtistic
co **N** siderate
in **D** ependent
funn **Y**

GA1082

Name Game—Consonant and Vowel Graph

This is a game of categories and matching beginning consonants and vowels. You may use your first name, last name, or a name you consider to be really challenging. Write the name at the top of the paper. Draw a graph chart under your name. Create categories such as those seen below. Add categories of interest such as books, restaurants, colors, garments, etc. Fill in each square that corresponds to the category and beginning letter. At the end of a designated time period, the challenge is open to the class to help those people who still have blank spaces on their charts. A challenge to the class might be: "Who can think of a food that starts with Y, a car that starts with E, a state that starts with O?" The objective is to fill in the entire graph.

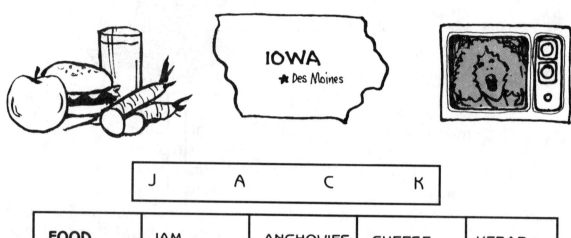

	J	A	C	K
FOOD	JAM	ANCHOVIES	CHEESE	KEBAB
STATES/ CITIES	JACKSON	ALASKA	COLORADO	KENTUCKY
TELEVISION	JOURNEY TO ADVENTURE	AMEN	CAPTAIN KANGAROO	KEYS TO SUCCESS
CARS	JAGUAR	ALPHA ROMEO	CHEVROLET	KAISER-FRASER
ANIMALS	JACKAL	ARMADILLO	COYOTE	KUDU

GA1082

Newspaper Contents

This activity is inspired by the national program NIE (Newspaper in Education)* and based upon the activities in a book entitled *Extra! Extra! Read All About It!*** For this partnership activity, ask the students to bring in the daily newspaper. If there are problems, give yourself enough lead time so that everyone has a copy of the same publication, printed on the same date. For orderly results, have the students staple the spine of the paper to keep it intact.

On the front page of the paper there will be an alphabetical list of the contents of the newspaper for that particular day. This may be called "Inside Today" or "Inside" or something similar. With a partner, look at the first item on the list. On our list we see "Ann Flanders" 2B which means Page 2, Section B. There may be some items with which you are not familiar. On our list what do you think "Bookmarks" means? (This is a feature dealing with new books on the market.)

---

*For more information about The Newspaper in Education Programs and NIE Week, contact your local newspaper, the International Reading Association or American Newspaper Publishers Association, Box 17407, Dulles Airport, Washington, D.C. 20041.

**Greta Lipson and Bernice Greenberg. *Extra! Extra! Read All About It! How to Use the Newspaper in the Classroom.* Carthage, Illinois: Good Apple, Inc., 1981.

GA1082

Having looked over your table of contents, start by finding the first item inside the newspaper. Call attention to other items on the same page. What is included in other columns? Now go back to the contents and find the second item on the correct page. Continue until you have examined every feature covered in the alphabetized contents. (For some students this may be their first comprehensive experience inside a complete newspaper.) Ask questions such as:

1. What section and page number are you looking at?
2. What articles do you see?
3. Who wrote them?
4. What are the articles about?
5. Scan the page for other interesting information.
6. What are the names of the sections of the newspaper?
   - Front Page
   - National and International News
   - Editorial Page
   - Sports
   - Comics
   - Advertising Throughout
   - Weather
   - Business
   - Classified Ads
   - Entertainment and Leisure
   - Daily Living

INSIDE TODAY

GA1082

Newspaper Treasure Hunt

Once again the student groups will be working with a complete newspaper (see preceding activity, Newspaper Contents). Before starting, have students select newspaper names for their groups. In order to play this game for points, the participants must be acquainted with the table of contents and be generally familiar with the sections of the newspaper.

Procedure:

The teacher will have a prepared list of items to be found for this Newspaper Treasure Hunt (length is optional). Cover the major sections of the paper. An example of questions would be:

1. Find the price of one pound of hamburger.
2. Find an editorial cartoon.
3. Find a business report.
4. Locate the horoscope for today.
5. Find the names of three politicians.
6. What is a basketball score for the home team?
7. Locate a used car for sale.
8. What is the biggest news on the front page?

MP ninth girls win 41-32, now 8-0 boys lose

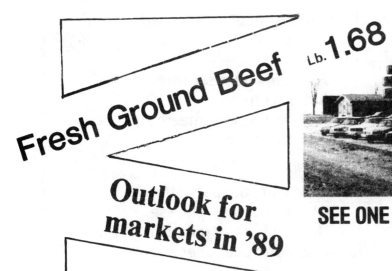

Fresh Ground Beef Lb. 1.68

Outlook for markets in '89

SEE ONE OF THESE FINE USED CARS

The group that locates each piece of information is scored one point for the team. Answers must be specific—including section, page and column. If the information is incorrect, the team receives a negative point. The teams may respond to one item at a time, as read by the teacher, or a treasure hunt list may be given to each group. The first group to finish is the winner. All answers must be checked against the newspaper before the final results are known.

Greta Lipson and Bernice Greenberg. *Extra! Extra! Read All About It! How to Use the Newspaper in the Classroom.* Carthage, Illinois: Good Apple, Inc., 1981.

GA1082

On Top of Spaghetti

"On Top of Spaghetti" is a parody of the original old Kentucky mountain song, "On Top of Old Smokey." A parody is the imitation of someone else's work and can treat a topic seriously or in a funny or ridiculous manner. If you want to try to write a parody, remember to acknowledge the original poet or song writer, composer or author. You may create your words to any kind of music, from Beethoven to the present day, with terrific results.

A parody can be difficult to write, but it is not at all difficult to sing this wonderful meatball song and leave the parody to someone else.

On Top of Spaghetti

On top of spa ghet ti   All covered with cheese,

I lost my poor meatball   When somebody sneezed.

It rolled off the table
And on to the floor,
And then my poor meatball
It rolled out the door.

And early next summer
It grew into a tree,
All covered with meatballs
All ready for me.

It rolled into the garden
And under a bush,
And then my poor meatball
Was nothing but mush.

So if you eat spaghetti
All covered with cheese,
Hold on to your meatball
And don't ever sneeze.

Glory, Glory, How Peculiar. Compiled by Charles Keller © 1976. Reprinted by permission of the publisher, Prentice-Hall, Inc., Englewood Cliffs, N.J.

106

Oxymoron: I Am Clearly Confused

Oxymoron! What a strange word! An oxymoron describes a combination of two contradictory words. The word derives from the Greek word *oxus* (sharp) and *moris* (stupid). We hear these combinations all the time and we understand them, too. But if we stop to think about them seriously, they are really quite weird. For example: "That hound dog is *pretty ugly.*" How can something be pretty and ugly at the same time? Can you explain these oxymorons? If you had never heard these expressions before, what would your reaction be to the speaker who used them?

1. The plant is growing smaller. (I thought growing means getting larger.)
2. My favorite flavor is bittersweet. (Make up your mind!)
3. Do you like jumbo shrimp? (What size do you mean—jumbo or shrimp?)
4. I would like a cold hot dog. (You must be kidding. Do you want it hot or cold?)
5. That was a cruel kindness.
6. It was a living death.
7. Let's pig out moderately.
8. The two of them are friendly enemies.
9. It was a peaceful war.
10. He's a little giant.

Can you think of an oxymoron which you have heard? Make up an oxymoron.

I MAY BE PRETTY UGLY, BUT I'M AWFUL NICE.

Pangram: Quick Brown Fox

Of course we all know about a verse, or a sentence, or a phrase that includes all the letters of the alphabet. This kind of statement is often used as a strategy in printing, handwriting, spelling or typing when we need a test of our skill. Our good old friend "The quick brown fox" is the pangram most commonly used, but perhaps it is time for a change. Can you think up a sentence that will include all twenty-six letters of the alphabet and serve the same purpose? Remember it must make sense and be something clever that people can remember.

The quick brown fox jumped over the lazy dog's back.

1. It may help to list words that use the most difficult letters in a pangram, such as *z x q k.* If a list is long enough, the task of developing a pangram that makes sense is more likely.

2. If you can't develop a pangram with real words that make sense, try a pangram with *pronounceable nonsense* words!

GA1082

Paper Bag Drama: Improvisation

On Monday, plan ahead for Paper Bag Dramas on Friday (or any day of your choice). Organize five groups of five students, or any variation that is workable. The students in each group are to decide upon items that each person will bring from home to be collected into their group paper shopping bag. At the same time they will plan and write out a simple drama as if they were going to use each item in the bag in a five to ten-minute improvisational performance.

On Friday, or the designated day, each group will bring in a bag filled with the planned objects and switch their bag of goodies with another group. Once again the groups will assemble, but this time they must examine the items in the "new" bag. From these odds and ends, they must write a brief description of the skit which they will enact. Every item in the bag must be used. Allow for rehearsal. As each group stands for their presentation, the title of the skit must be written on the chalkboard. (The class may also want a list of the items the actors are working with.)

When the play is over, the originators of the bag are to tell the class, briefly, what *their* group had planned as a skit based upon the objects. Was there a great difference in the scenarios?

All of the articles in the bag need not be related—in many ways that creates a more challenging task. The items must be large enough, however, to be seen effectively in a performance in front of an audience. A paper clip would not be acceptable.

Example of paper bag items:

A headband
An alarm clock
A clipboard

A sweat sock
An eggbeater

GA1082

Parts of Speech for Sports

Because there is so much colorful language and action in sports reporting, the sports section of the newspaper supplies great raw material for this activity. With a supply of newspapers on hand, select a brief article and delete the nouns, verbs and adjectives of your choice. Then in front of the room, ask the class to supply the deleted words for you. It is allowable to offer clues to the type of nouns, verbs and adjectives that would fit. For example: "Give me a noun that is part of the body," Write the new words in place as they are suggested by your classmates and then read your story with the new words. Accept only the words that are strong and imaginative; you can refuse the words that are pale and lifeless—the laughs are bigger that way.

1. A noun names a person, place or thing. A proper noun names a particular person, place or thing: Sue Smith, Boston, Sparkle Polish
2. A verb is a word expressing action.
3. An adjective is a describing word.

For example:

Hockey

Hockey is a (violent) game. A lot of fans think it
       adjective
should be controlled by the (leagues). There are
                       plural noun
(crushing) body checks, and free-for-all (fights).
adjective   plural noun
Last week (Sandy) McNertney, a member of the
         proper noun
(Podunk) Pistols, punched a patron in the (nose)
proper noun   noun-part of the body
because the patron stole his hockey stick.

McNertney chased the thief with a (wet) (towel)
                       adjective noun
right up to the (refreshment) stand and (knocked)
             noun-type of food   verb (past tense)
him to the floor. Another player removed the

patron's (shoe) and bounced it off his (head). Then
      noun   noun-part of the body
the (angry) player (ran) and grabbed him by his
   adjective   verb (past tense)
(skinny) throat. This is not a (funny) story. Let's
adjective   adjective
take the violence out of hockey. It will make us

(better) fans and (better) players. It's no joke!
adjective   adjective

Greta Lipson and Bernice Greenberg. *Extra! Extra! Read All About It! How to Use the Newspaper in the Classroom.* Carthage, Illinois: Good Apple, Inc., 1981.

GA1082

Pen Pals: Write to K-2

Inform the k-2 teachers in your school or district that your upper grade students will answer letters which have been written (or dictated) by their k-2 pupils. An ideal time for this exchange to take place is at holiday time. Your older students may send messages to include:

1. Halloween fun and safety messages
2. Thanksgiving regards and Pilgrim and Indian regards
3. News from Santa's helpers in the North Pole workshops (no gift requests, please)

4. Hanukkah greetings on the Festival of Lights
5. A Groundhog Day report and explanation
6. Valentine's Day greetings

7. St. Patrick's Day four-leaf clovers
8. April Fool's humorous messages
9. Easter Bunny regards

10. Memorial Day holiday wishes
11. Flag Day greetings
12. New Year's greetings

These letters will be personal and full of color and good cheer. They will also be accurately produced messages with good spelling and grammar. All letters will be read by the teacher as a final check point before being sent out. Every k-2 pupil who sent a letter will receive a reply on stationery that has been especially illustrated to reflect the spirit of the holiday. This is purposeful writing that enhances the self-esteem of older students who are doing something gracious and caring to make little kids happy!

GA1082

Polysemy: Multiple Meanings for One Word

There are some simple words that have multiple meanings which we use in everyday conversation. If someone asks for an example of these words, it is difficult to remember. For that reason this exercise is a good group activity. As the ideas come from the class, the whole exercise picks up momentum and we begin to recall these ordinary words that are used in a variety of ways. These particular words are spelled the same, no matter how they are used. How many can you think of?

Spread:
1. A bird can spread his wings.
2. I love sandwich spread on my bread.
3. The bedspread has flowers on it.
4. The spread sheet comes off the computer.
5. Spread the news around the school.
6. She lives on a vast spread of farmland.
7. The spread in the test scores is surprising.
8. The restaurant put on a delicious picnic spread.

Suggested words: run—fast—sound—stick—medium—spring
The class may want to keep this list handy in the classroom for later additions.

GA1082

Positive Me from A to Z

Use every letter in the alphabet to describe who you are, what your interests are, and what you are all about. If you come to a letter that stops you, skip over it for a while and return to it later. You may use sentences or phrases, and you may start with any word of your choice, as long as you use and underline the alphabetical word in its consecutive place.

Example:
A I am an <u>athlete</u>.
B often called a <u>baseball</u> nut
C my voice can be heard in the <u>chorus</u>
D stands for <u>dedication</u> to my stamp collection
E well-known as the most <u>eager</u> summer camper
F a loyal <u>friend</u> to my buddy
G everybody knows I'm a <u>go-getter</u>
H <u>handy</u> in the kitchen
I my poetry <u>inspires</u> others
J they say I'm a <u>joker</u>
K <u>kind</u> to others
L friendly and <u>likeable</u>, that's me!
M I always try to remember good <u>manners</u>
N know when to say <u>no</u>!
O <u>outstanding</u> talent for music
P <u>patient</u> with little kids
Q <u>quick</u> at math
R love to <u>read</u> a good book
S <u>shy</u> when in crowds
T as <u>tactful</u> as possible
U <u>understanding</u> to a fault
V <u>vulnerable</u> where animals are concerned
W a <u>warmhearted</u> person
X never learned to play the <u>xylophone</u>
Y have a <u>yen</u> for <u>yummy</u> desserts
Z crazy about the <u>zoo</u>

GA1082

Postcard Awards: Pat on the Back

Discuss achievement, effort, cooperation, kindness, tenacity, and all those qualities that are valued in class by teachers and students. Adopt a class motto that announces to the school and community exactly what your class stands for. Example: *Pride in effort and cooperation*!

Have the students contribute the price of stamped postcards which they will address in class to their parents or guardians. Research business logos in your city. Pay particular attention to the ones that are successful and easily recognized. Make a logo from the class motto at the bottom of the postcard. A volunteer who prints well can do this carefully, or the district print shop may be able to help. These logos will then be put on file for future use as "Postcard Awards."

Let every student know that at least once during the semester the teacher will send a personal postcard home expressing pride in each student's performance at school. This may be an acknowledgment of good citizenship, academic excellence, attitude or outstanding effort!

Investigate the cost of having buttons made with the class logo that can be pinned to students' shirts. (A logo is an advertiser's trademark. Think about the fast food logos that are so familiar to consumers.) School districts often have button-making machines.

GA1082

Progressive Story

A progressive story is a creative activity for total class participation. Each person in the room makes a contribution sequentially. If the Progressive Story is recorded on cassette, it can be fun. The class can recapture the humor of the event and identify the voices of classmates. The teacher can start telling a story. At a climactic place or a logical changing point, the teller switches to the next person, either in order of seats or, to make it more exciting, at the whim of the storyteller. Depending on the time and the number of students, each person will take between thirty seconds and a minute. Make sure the person who is to end the narrative is aware that he/she can wrap up the story.

Example:

First person: It was a drenching, beastly night. Thunder and lightning tore the skies apart to the steady hum of my windshield wipers. My dog Shark and I strained to see through the windshield as my faithful car coughed, sputtered and died on the road. What a place to be. Through the mist I could barely see a stately old mansion. We hunched our shoulders against the wind and arrived at the heavy oak door when all of a sudden . . . .

Remember, the story can take any turn you want it to. You may add characters, but don't forget the old ones. Any additions in the plot (story map) must make sense; you wouldn't want to go from the scene above into a supermarket aisle. Warning! People who don't know when to stop may be pulled out of the room by a hook.

GA1082

Proverbs Rephrased

A proverb is a short traditional saying that makes a strong statement which most people accept as the truth. It may also be called a pithy saying, a maxim or an adage (all adages are old). A proverb hits the nail on the head because we understand the figurative language instantly without going into a long-winded explanation of what it means. In many cases it is our experience that helps us understand. But how difficult would it be to rewrite an adage if you were not permitted to use the same words?

Test your skills by rewriting the following proverbs. See if others are able to recognize them. Since you must use synonyms, it would be helpful to refer to a thesaurus. You can be extravagant, mysterious or straightforward as long as you produce a *literal* translation. You may even want to use proverbs from your memory, after working with the list below.

Example:
1. A rolling stone gathers no moss. (A sphere that keeps moving does not attract any soft, green velvety plants on its surface.)
2. You can't teach an old dog new tricks. (An aged canine cannot be instructed with fresh lessons.)
3. When in Rome, do as the Romans do.
4. The grass is always greener on the other side of the fence.
5. Look before you leap.
6. Too many cooks spoil the broth.
7. All that glitters is not gold.
8. Don't cry over spilled milk.
9. People who live in glass houses shouldn't throw stones.
10. You can lead a horse to water, but you can't make him drink.
11. A stitch in time saves nine.
12. All work and no play makes Jack a dull boy.
13. Every cloud has a silver lining.
14. The squeaky wheel gets the grease.
15. Haste makes waste.
16. Don't count your chickens before they hatch.

Duplicate this list for the class. The students may read their rewritten statements and invite the class to identify the original proverbs.

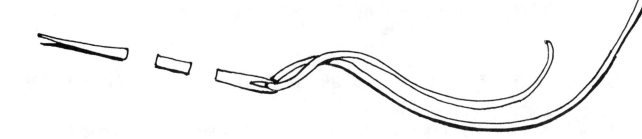

GA1082

Proverbs Explained

In the preceding activity, Proverbs Rephrased, the task was to rewrite a proverb *literally*, using synonyms. ("Dead men tell no tales" rephrased becomes—"Male cadavers are incapable of yielding any testimony.") It is possible to translate in that fashion without understanding the meaning of the proverb. As a challenge to your powers of analysis, review the figurative language of the proverbs below, in the left column. Connect the proverb at the left with its appropriate explanation on the right. Be careful—there are fifteen proverbs and sixteen meanings. This can be done individually or as an oral exercise with the entire class working from the following duplicated list:

Proverbs:

1. The grass is always greener on the other side of the fence.
2. Look before you leap.
3. Too many cooks spoil the broth.
4. Every cloud has a silver lining.
5. Don't count your chickens before they hatch.
6. Let sleeping dogs lie.
7. Haste makes waste.
8. All that glitters is not gold.
9. People who live in glass houses shouldn't throw stones.
10. Don't cry over spilled milk.
11. You can't teach an old dog new tricks.
12. When in Rome, do as the Romans do.
13. The pen is mightier than the sword.
14. A bird in the hand is worth two in the bush.
15. All good things come to those who wait.

Meanings:

A. You can't be certain about the outcome of events.
B. Things that look good may not be good.
C. Everyone has faults (including you) so don't criticize.
D. It's all over so forget it.
E. What you can't have often looks better than what you have.
F. Too many people on one task may make things worse.
G. Be careful before you get into something.
H. Things are not always as bad as they look.
I. If things are quiet, don't stir up trouble.
J. A job done too quickly may turn out so poorly that it must be done over.
K. When you are in a strange situation, watch how others act and behave accordingly.
L. A proverb is to speech what salt is to food.
M. Patience is rewarded.
N. Older people resist new ideas.
O. It's better to be certain with what you have than to gamble for more.
P. Ideas have more power than brute strength.

Addendum:

We didn't say proverbs are true; we just said they are often accepted as the truth. Which of these above would you protest? Give your reasons!

Answers: 1E, 2G, 3F, 4H, 5A, 6I, 7J, 8B, 9C, 10D, 11N, 12K, 13P, 14O, 15M

Greta Lipson and Jane Romatowski. *Ethnic Pride*. Carthage, Illinois: Good Apple, Inc., 1983.

Rhopalics: I Do Too

Rhopalon is a Greek word that describes a club which is slender at the handle and thickens and gets wider toward the head. That brings us to the term *rhopalic*, which also describes something in language that increases in size. A rhopalic is a sentence, verse, phrase, or paragraph in which each successive word has one more letter than the last or, in another form, has one more syllable with each additional word. Of course, it must all make sense and that's a big problem. Try this maddening stunt yourself. Select each word in a sentence with one more letter, or try it with increasing syllables. To make life easier with the former (increasing letters), we suggest you use some connecting words to help out. If you can manage without them, try it with your rhopalic!

Increase Each Word by One Letter:

1	2	3	4	5	6	—	7	—	8	1	2	3
I	do	see	this	silly	effort	as	painful	and	annoying.	I	do	too!

Increase Syllables: A Nonrhyming Poem or Statement

1	2	3	4
The	sergeant	entreated	Emmanuel

1	2	3	4
To	muster	citizens	vigorously

1	2	3	4
For	battles	converting	patriotic

1	2	3	4
Pride	into	national	security.

In order to reduce the difficulty of this exercise, organize a Word Squad whose job it is to organize lists of words by syllable and letter count. Remember the first grade technique of clapping out a word to count the syllables. Have someone at the chalkboard as the entire class composes a rhopalic.

GA1082

Robot Art: Draw What I Describe

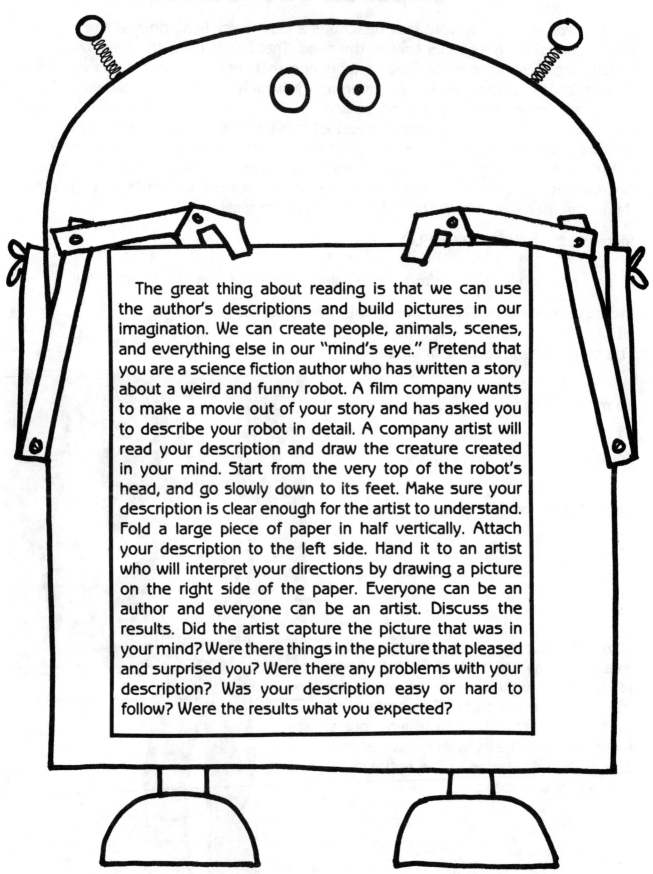

The great thing about reading is that we can use the author's descriptions and build pictures in our imagination. We can create people, animals, scenes, and everything else in our "mind's eye." Pretend that you are a science fiction author who has written a story about a weird and funny robot. A film company wants to make a movie out of your story and has asked you to describe your robot in detail. A company artist will read your description and draw the creature created in your mind. Start from the very top of the robot's head, and go slowly down to its feet. Make sure your description is clear enough for the artist to understand. Fold a large piece of paper in half vertically. Attach your description to the left side. Hand it to an artist who will interpret your directions by drawing a picture on the right side of the paper. Everyone can be an author and everyone can be an artist. Discuss the results. Did the artist capture the picture that was in your mind? Were there things in the picture that pleased and surprised you? Were there any problems with your description? Was your description easy or hard to follow? Were the results what you expected?

GA1082

Role Play: Little Acts

Role play, sometimes called improvisational drama, is an entertaining way of developing oral language skills and ease in front of others. Characters may be drawn from familiar folktales, myths, modern stories read in class, or they may be taken from cameo situations with evocative content for interpretation. Practice helps students understand and feel comfortable with role play and each experience makes it easier. There is no right or wrong way to assume a role. Students may develop characters according to their own perception and style which makes the enterprise more venturesome.

Here is a strategy for warming up the class and demonstrating the technique. These are sample situations with no familiar clues.

The teacher will say to the class, in a neutral tone of voice, "Mary has changed."

Now the teacher will choose respondents who, one at a time, assume the following roles: Mother, Father, Girlfriend, Teacher, Boyfriend. Give each character a chance to react to the statement, which may be repeated for effect. After the first experience, emphasize that responses may be both negative and positive. Don't imitate others! Express your own point of view!

Other Starters:
1. Mary has changed.
2. Nobody wants Wimpy on the team.
   Coach
   Student
   Good player
   Teacher
   Friend
3. Ginny is always perfect.
   Brother
   Enemy
   Neighbor
   Employer
   Counselor
4. Everybody picks on Wilber.
   Gym teacher
   Cousin
   Grandfather
   School bus driver
   Girlfriend
5. Company is coming to dinner.
   Mother
   Family dog
   Grandpa
   Baby sister
   Big brother

Greta Lipson and Baxter Morrison. *Fact, Fantasy and Folklore*. Carthage, Illinois: Good Apple, Inc., 1977.

GA1082

Roman Numerals

Roman numerals are written with seven basic symbols: I (1), V (5), X (10), L (50), C (100), D (500) and M (1000). All other numbers are a combination of these seven symbols, except for numbers beginning with four or nine. Roman numerals use the principle of addition. For example, twenty-five is written XXV (10 + 10 + 5). The numbers four and nine, and any numbers beginning with four or nine, use the principle of subtraction. For example, four is written IV (5 – 1) and ninety is written XC (100 – 10). To solve the arithmetic problems below, first convert the Roman numerals into Arabic numbers. Can you write the answers in Roman numerals?

1. $\begin{array}{r} VIII = \text{\underline{\hspace{2cm}}} \\ \times\ V = \times \text{\underline{\hspace{2cm}}} \\ \hline XL = \text{\underline{\hspace{2cm}}} \end{array}$

2. $\begin{array}{r} XXXIII = \text{\underline{\hspace{2cm}}} \\ +\ XVII = + \text{\underline{\hspace{2cm}}} \\ \hline L = \text{\underline{\hspace{2cm}}} \end{array}$

3. $\begin{array}{r} LXIX = \text{\underline{\hspace{2cm}}} \\ -\ XI = - \text{\underline{\hspace{2cm}}} \\ \hline LVIII = \text{\underline{\hspace{2cm}}} \end{array}$

4. $\begin{array}{r} C = \text{\underline{\hspace{2cm}}} \\ CX = \text{\underline{\hspace{2cm}}} \\ +\ CXL = + \text{\underline{\hspace{2cm}}} \\ \hline CCCL = \text{\underline{\hspace{2cm}}} \end{array}$

5. $\begin{array}{r} MMM = \text{\underline{\hspace{2cm}}} \\ -\ MDCC = - \text{\underline{\hspace{2cm}}} \\ \hline MCCC = \text{\underline{\hspace{2cm}}} \end{array}$

6. $\begin{array}{r} CMXCIX = \text{\underline{\hspace{2cm}}} \\ -\ III = \div \text{\underline{\hspace{2cm}}} \\ \hline CCCXXXIII = \text{\underline{\hspace{2cm}}} \end{array}$

7. $\begin{array}{r} DCCXVIII = \text{\underline{\hspace{2cm}}} \\ -\ CLXXXVII = - \text{\underline{\hspace{2cm}}} \\ \hline DXXXI = \text{\underline{\hspace{2cm}}} \end{array}$

8. $\begin{array}{r} DLXXV = \text{\underline{\hspace{2cm}}} \\ +\ MMDCXLIV = + \text{\underline{\hspace{2cm}}} \\ \hline MMMCCXIX = \text{\underline{\hspace{2cm}}} \end{array}$

To write numbers larger than 3999, a bar is placed over a number to show that it is multiplied by 1000. For example, 5000 is written $\overline{V}$ (5 × 1000) and 4000 is written $M\overline{V}$ (5000–1000). How would you write the following numbers in Roman numerals?

1. 10,000 _____
2. 25,000 _____
3. 50,000 _____
4. 100,000 _____
5. 1,000,000 _____

6. 5,000,000 _____
7. 10,000,000 _____
8. 13,524 _____
9. Can you write the following number in Arabic numerals?
MMMMMMMMMMDCCCLXXXIV

_____

"A Romp with Roman Numerals" by Kelly Riley, *Oasis* reproducible page, Jan./ Feb. 1986 © Good Apple, Inc. Permission given by Good Apple, Inc.

Rules for Teachers in 1872

Duplicate Rules for Teachers so that everyone can consider all items for discussion. Pretend that you are applying for a teaching job in 1872 and are given this list so that you know exactly what is expected of you as a teacher. What questions do you have as you read this document? What objections do you have? What, in your opinion, is reasonable or unreasonable about these expectations? What, if anything, surprises you about this job description? Remember that these were authentic standards for hiring teachers in American communities in 1872.

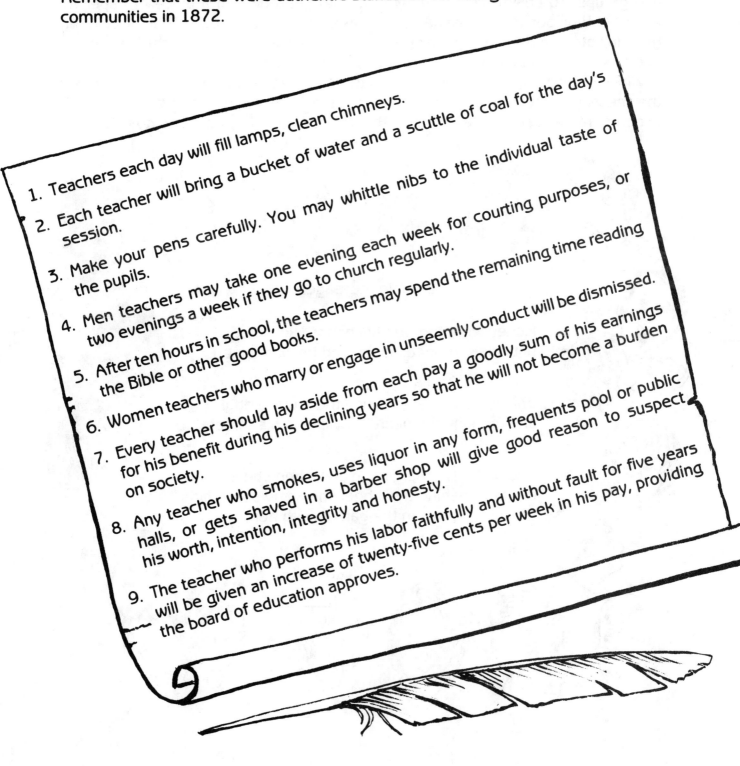

1. Teachers each day will fill lamps, clean chimneys.

2. Each teacher will bring a bucket of water and a scuttle of coal for the day's session.

3. Make your pens carefully. You may whittle nibs to the individual taste of the pupils.

4. Men teachers may take one evening each week for courting purposes, or two evenings a week if they go to church regularly.

5. After ten hours in school, the teachers may spend the remaining time reading the Bible or other good books.

6. Women teachers who marry or engage in unseemly conduct will be dismissed.

7. Every teacher should lay aside from each pay a goodly sum of his earnings for his benefit during his declining years so that he will not become a burden on society.

8. Any teacher who smokes, uses liquor in any form, frequents pool or public halls, or gets shaved in a barber shop will give good reason to suspect his worth, intention, integrity and honesty.

9. The teacher who performs his labor faithfully and without fault for five years will be given an increase of twenty-five cents per week in his pay, providing the board of education approves.

GA1082

Rumor Mill: Spread the News

Rumors and gossip are not to be trusted. There is no way to know where the information comes from or how it got started. By the time these stories circulate they have been changed, misunderstood and dramatized. Because gossip and rumors are unreliable, and not factual, they can be hurtful and are sometimes dangerous.

To demonstrate how "word of mouth" can be distorted, divide the class into two groups. To ensure accuracy, write a brief sentence on a piece of paper for yourself. Whisper the message to one person in each group. That person will then initiate the activity by whispering the exact message into the ear of the one next to him until everyone has acquired the information.

When both groups are finished, ask the last person in each group to repeat the message. How much difference was there from the original? How does this experiment parallel real life? Discuss the implications of rumors and gossip.

Sample messages:

Money went through his hands like water,
until his career collapsed and he was ruined.

*****

Shirley bent over to touch the stuffed dog
and thought she heard growling in his throat.

*****

She parked in the garage and when she slipped
out from behind the wheel she knew something
threatening was in the garage with her!

GA1082

Scrapbook for the Future

Prepare a gift for yourself by making a scrapbook which will be an entertaining and informative book in your future. As an adult, it is always fascinating to look back at your youthful days and recall details of your life and environment as a child. If you put some serious thought into it, a scrapbook will answer a variety of questions in later years. Collect newspapers and magazines of all kinds for cutting out pictures. Each page of your scrapbook will feature a picture that reflects the times you live in now! You should write your own commentary at the bottom of each picture page. For example: "I loved to eat a custard cream in a sugar cone that cost $1.00. Bubble gum flavor was the very best!" or "The guys all wore an earring in one ear. I didn't want to wear it because I thought it looked stupid, but I told the guys my father wouldn't let me!" or "We ate lots of hamburger in those days. Mom said it was the best buy at $1.29 a pound," or "The girls in my crowd wear ankle socks with ruffles. With high heels it's a killer combination."

Some of the picture information you collect will provide the following details when you are twenty, twenty-five or even forty years old.

1. Clothing styles for men, women and children and adolescents
2. Hair styles
3. Shoes
4. Automobiles (styles and prices)
5. Styles of houses, prices in your neighborhood
6. Apartment or house rental costs
7. Home interiors (especially the kitchen)
8. Entertainment of all kinds: movies, concerts, theater
9. Popular songs of the day and popular groups
10. Your favorite TV shows
11. Politics—who is running for what office in the city, state and nation
12. What news is big in the headlines?
13. Technology
14. Latest dance craze
15. Athletes and teams
16. How much does a candy bar cost? What does it weigh?

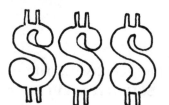

This is just a partial list. Your scrapbook will be personal and should emphasize your tastes as well as what's going on in the world. Take your time in developing this scrapbook. You will be crazy about it in ten years! Share the results with your class.

GA1082

Sentences: Declarative, Imperative, Etc.

On the chalkboard write the names of the four types of sentences and describe the message each type communicates.

A *declarative sentence* makes a statement.

I like you.
Pie is good.

An *imperative sentence* makes commands.

Pick up the junk in your room, Buster, or it will be the end for you.
Carry those garbage cans to the curb and make it snappy.

An *interrogative sentence* asks a question.

Do you call that singing?
Will the rain hurt the rhubarb?

An *exclamatory sentence* is an expression of surprise or strong emotion.

Holy smokes, the cow jumped over the moon!
She slammed that homer right over the fence!

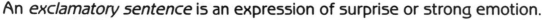

The class activity can be a four-team effort (the declarative team, imperative team, interrogative team and exclamatory team). Using assorted reading materials in the classroom, the teams will find as many sentences in a given time sequence as they can, recording the sentences as they discover them. Or, as a whole class effort, people at their seats can search for the assigned types of sentences required on the board. Asking students to make up sharp and funny sentences of their own invention is another interesting route to take.

GA1082

Sentences out of Context

In the book, *A Dictionary of Reading and Related Terms* edited by Harris and Hodges, International Reading Association, Newark, Delaware, 1981, *context* is defined as "the set of circumstances that surround a spoken or written message and form a framework for its interpretation."

The following strange sentences have actually been spoken by someone in some context. What do you think they could possibly mean? Do the best you can to explain something about the context of these statements. If you also have a favorite sentence, you may ask the class to develop the context. Briefly, what story or situation is the setting for these remarks?

1. My brother stuffed macaroni in his nose!
2. I'm telling you a dog answered the phone.
3. The divers go down to a telephone booth in Stony Lake.
4. She said she would drop in through the roof.
5. The computer has a girlfriend.
6. The lawn hose is sticking out of a hole in the ground, and we can't pull it out!
7. My fortune cookie said, "Go to Hollywood, you need the walk."
8. The garbage truck swallowed the entire dumpster.
9. The skunk got his head caught in a bottle and we needed help!
10. He fell into a vat of chocolate milk and almost drowned.
11. The machine had real eyes.
12. "Good heavens, General—they have sent in the fuzzy wuzzy reinforcements."
13. The sausage machine kept cranking away covering the floor with hot dogs.
14. She thought she was picking a peach off the tree and it turned out to be a bat hanging upside down!
15. She followed the cookbook directions, made a hole in the potato, stuck in a hot dog and baked it till it was black.
16. The table was set for a special dinner and the little dog hopped up on the fancy cloth and walked across all the dishes, food and silverware.
17. The mouse had babies right on the candy counter and nobody knew what to do.
18. I was sitting at a very fancy dinner, and pointing to the turkey I said to the hostess, "Pass the garbage!"

GA1082

Shipwreck: Role Play

Directions to the Teacher:

The good ship *Intrepid* is sinking and the life rafts with the children are already safely afloat. There is a good chance that all the survivors—children and adults—will reach Bounty Island which has vegetation and will support life. The captain must decide which of the remaining adult passengers are critical to the survival of the group and will be allowed to board the last life raft. The captain must be included since he is the only navigator. Five worthy people must be selected from the ten who wait at the rail. The captain (represented by the class) will listen to the reasons why each person feels he/she should be included among the survivors. Each will describe the contribution he/she is able to make to the group on Bounty Island, once they arrive and settle down.

Each character stands or is seated in front of the class with a printed sign identifying the role being played. Each one defends his/her importance to the general welfare. Later each character responds to questions or arguments about his/her contribution that will be made for survival. The members at the rail may also have conversation among themselves. The class represents the embodiment of the captain. Each class member listens and makes the crucial decision just as the captain must.

After the session each class member must submit a list of the five people chosen to go on the raft with reasons for the choices. Reasons for excluding the other five people must be included as well. Tally the results. Which five among the ten have been selected to go with the children and the captain to Bounty Island?

Role Play Parts

Remember that you want to stay alive. To go on the raft means to live—to be left behind means to die. Be convincing! These parts are not to be read aloud or memorized! Privately hand the clues on the following pages for role play to the characters. These are only clues. The characters should embellish their parts with imagination.

1. Minister: You can give spiritual comfort in time of need.
2. Doctor: You can care for those who may be injured or ill.
3. Mechanic: You can fix or build anything.
4. Ocean Scientist: You know a great deal about the ocean, its creatures and vegetation.
5. Farmer: You have the skill to make things grow under all conditions.
6. Judge: You can settle disputes because of your law training.

7. Sports Hero: You are a very good organizer. You will be able to set up leisure time activities for recreation.
8. Journalist: You will keep a written history of this ordeal for the world.
9. Teacher: Only you can teach the shipwrecked children on the island. They will need the benefits of learning so they will not turn into little savages.
10. Movie Star: You are a world famous entertainer. You can sing and dance and make people happy! Everybody needs something for their spirit, to make them laugh and feel life is worth living.

Greta Lipson and Baxter Morrison. *Fact, Fantasy and Folklore.* Carthage, Illinois: Good Apple, Inc., 1977.

GA1082

Similes: Like a Red Apple

When writers want to describe something in a vivid way, they will use similes. A simile is a figure of speech which compares two unlike things that share a special quality. If a writer wants you to really see—in your mind's eye—the blue of the sea, he may compare blue sea and sapphires. Blue seas and sapphires are quite a bit different, but they share "blueness." In creating a simile, the writer will use linking words such as *like, as, similar to, resembles* in order to paint a word picture.

"The blue sea gleamed like sapphires in the sun."

Try to write some similes yourself by completing the chart below. You will find this to be a handy tool as you write your own stories and poems.

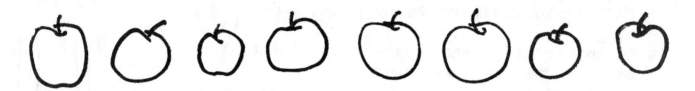

Nouns	Action Words	Comparing Words	Similes
1. dog	ate	machine	The dog ate like a machine.
2. popcorn			
3. mosquito			
4. shark			
5. night			
6. gum			
7. storm			
8. snow			
9. robot			
10. boxer			
11. crowd			
12. speedboat			

Greta Lipson and Jane A. Romatowski. *Calliope: A Handbook of 47 Poetic Forms.* Carthage, Illinois: Good Apple, Inc., 1981.

GA1082

Spelling Baseball

Prepare a list of spelling
words which range from easy to difficult,
or prepare a list of commonly misspelled words, or
category words taken from space, sports, food products,
"computereze," or student choices. This word list goes to the
pitcher of each team in turn. Name the two teams for identity
and easier management. These teams could be the "Yahoos" and
the "Rutabagas."

Ask for volunteers for two teams. Establish the position of home
plate, first, second and third bases. Put a chair in each spot for the players.
The Yahoos are first up to bat and they are ready and lined up at home
plate. The pitcher for the Rutabagas calls the batter to the chalkboard and
pronounces the first word which is on his spelling list. The batter must
write the word on the board spelled correctly and legibly. If the word
is correct, the batter proceeds to first base; if not, the umpire
yells, "You're out."

Just as in a real baseball game—the player on first
base proceeds around the bases if the spellers on the
team are accurate and get hits. If the Yahoos strike
out three times, the Rutabagas are then up to
bat. The game is won by the team with
the most runs!

This game can be adapted to any other skills subject with equal success. Coaching
the players is strictly forbidden, but encouragement and cheering is allowed.

GA1082

Spelling Scramble

Each member of the class is given the following list of sentences in which the spelling of one word is scrambled! A strong clue to the mystery word as it should appear when unscrambled is found in the context of the sentence. *Context* means the surrounding parts of the sentence or statement that help explain the total meaning and help identify the scrambled word.

The sentences may be written on the board, as an alternative, with all eyes front, and brains in place, as everyone tries to unscramble the words.

The task can be much more difficult with two mystery words in a sentence. An entire sentence with each word scrambled is really a mind-bender. Try writing one! Give one oral clue.

1. *Nslioilm* of dollars were spent on roads. (Millions)
2. Stormy Midwest was hit by *rnotdaeso*. (tornadoes)
3. The camping *rpti* was a great success. (trip)
4. A sports *rnaea* was built for the home team. (arena)
5. *Ahwt eosd lingleps aenm*? (What does spelling mean?)

Add some of your own scrambled sentences.

For another similar exercise, see Sentences out of Context.

GA1082

Spoonerisms
A Sunny Flip of the Tongue

There is a funny slip of the tongue which is called a "spoonerism." This particular form is named after William Archibald Spooner (1844-1930), an English reverend who taught at New College, Oxford, England. Spooner is said to have delighted his students at lectures because of his amusing turn of speech, which was an unintentional transposition of sounds. He usually interchanged the initial consonants of words so that "A well oiled bicycle" became "A well boiled icycle." "Conquering kings" became "Kinkering congs." After so many years we still appreciate this comic form. To enjoy this experience yourself, select a Mother Goose rhyme, a poem, recipe, folktale, or anything you think would work well. Begin by writing down your selection and experimenting.
Here is an example from Mother Goose.

"Hey, Diddle, Diddle"
(Someone was flaying a piddle!)

Original:
    Hey, diddle, diddle!
    The cat and the fiddle
    The cow jumped over the moon
    The little dog laughed
    To see such fun
    And the dish ran away with the spoon
    Yes, the dish ran away with the spoon!

Spoonerism:
    Dey, hiddle, diddle!
    The fat and the ciddle
    The jow cumped mover the oon
    The dittle log laughed
    To fee such sun
    And the rish dan away spith the woon
    Yes, the rish dan away spith the woon!

HA HA HA! THIS IS FOO TUNNY!

OH, HELP! I AM FOING to GALL!

How about trying:
    "Loldi Gocks and the Bree Thears"
    "Sumpty Wumpty hat on a dall"
    "Pinderella and the lood cooking grince"

Remember, whenever you remove the beginning consonant or consonant blend of a word, you must exchange it with the beginning consonant of another word.

GA1082

Sports Word Search

For you sports enthusiasts who can never get enough challenges, here is a different test of sporting skills.

Directions: The words must always be in a straight line. Never skip a letter. The words may run forward, backward, up, down, diagonally.

```
A  R  C  H  E  R  Y  L  L  A  B  T  O  O  F
T  M  A  R  K  C  R  I  C  K  E  T  P  Q  S
R  Q  G  S  T  E  V  E  U  A  Z  Q  G  I  A
A  N  N  R  A  U  T  O  R  A  C  I  N  G  Y
C  K  I  U  T  F  L  Z  L  O  A  N  G  G  B
K  Z  L  G  O  L  F  X  I  Y  E  K  C  O  H
J  G  T  B  A  D  M  I  N  T  O  N  C  J  D
O  N  S  Y  A  S  X  G  G  N  I  H  S  I  F
G  I  E  H  T  S  O  G  N  I  T  A  K  S  I
G  F  R  L  Q  N  E  C  Z  I  J  D  H  R  S
I  R  W  U  J  N  B  B  C  X  L  E  U  P  K
N  U  A  T  E  R  G  G  A  E  E  W  M  I  I
G  S  A  I  L  I  N  G  W  L  R  N  O  Q  I
H  V  V  O  L  L  E  Y  B  A  L  L  L  B  N
S  W  I  M  M  I  N  G  H  U  N  T  I  N  G
```

Clues:

hockey	badminton	soccer	baseball	fishing
tennis	volleyball	track	curling	swimming
sailing	squash	cricket	golf	football
bowling	skating	skiing	hunting	auto racing
wrestling	jogging	archery	surfing	rugby

Greta Lipson and Bernice Greenberg. *Extra! Extra! Read All About It! How to Use the Newspaper in the Classroom.* Carthage, Illinois: Good Apple, Inc., 1981.

Stream of Consciousness: Word Connections

Sometimes we hear or read a word that stimulates a great rush of ideas and feelings that we associate with that particular word. The words and concepts that we "free associate" are unique to each of us. It can be fascinating to ask a person to explain where the word connections come from and what they mean to the individual. (They may not always know themselves.) Start with one strong word to use as a heading on the chalkboard that will inspire student participation.

Some heading suggestions:

Homework   Chocolate cake   State fair
Dreams   Science fiction   Comedy
Athlete   Popcorn   Dancing

Use one or more headings at a time to start the ideas moving. People at their seats should copy the headings from the board and list the words they personally contribute. When the board is full of free word associations, start asking questions of those who volunteered the words.

For example:
Under the heading "Popcorn"—who said *Indians*? Why does popcorn remind you of Indians? (Because Indians introduced popcorn to the Pilgrims.)

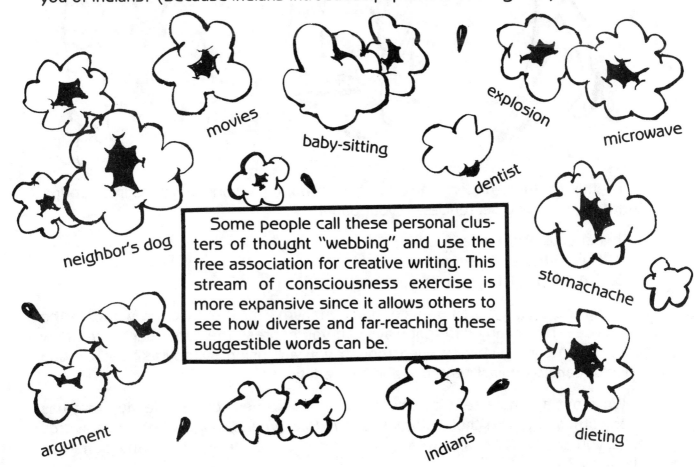

movies

baby-sitting

explosion

microwave

dentist

neighbor's dog

Some people call these personal clusters of thought "webbing" and use the free association for creative writing. This stream of consciousness exercise is more expansive since it allows others to see how diverse and far-reaching these suggestible words can be.

stomachache

argument

Indians

dieting

GA1082

Synonyms: Thesaurus

How did you come into class this morning? Did you sashay, stumble, galumph, mince or slink? Anybody can just plain "walk" in, but if you look in the thesaurus, you have a choice of all kinds of words that can also describe the act of walking. The thesaurus is a resource which provides synonyms. A synonym is a word that is *somewhat* similar in meaning to another word. But in the English language there are not many words that have *exactly* the same meaning as another word.

WALK?

Try this for more understanding of how synonyms work. Organize into groups. Write the following sentences on your paper:

1. I *cried* at the movie.
2. My mother *hollered* at me.
3. Did the politician *lie* to the people?

Using the thesaurus as a guide, find synonyms for the italicized words in the sentences. How many different ways can you express the same sentence? How does the meaning change even though you are using synonyms? Each group should read its original sentence and the variations.

Write out a simple sentence centered around a verb or an adjective that has many other synonym choices: *golden, ill, kid, command, laugh, cheat.* What words take you the farthest and what synonyms change the intent of the sentence the most?

GA1082

Tall Tales

Tall tales are among the most popular stories in the history of storytelling. Both children and adults are captivated by them. These tales have no historical credibility but are wonderfully wild accounts of American folk heroes. Some people call tall tales folklore and others call them "fake lore" because these powerful heroes in these stories perform superhuman feats as they swagger and boast through their adventures. Each story represents a male or female hero with a special regional flair. The heroes may be farmers, sailors, riverboat captains, cowboys, lumberjacks, or others born of industry and new frontiers in America. In recognition of these endearing heroes, set aside time for a student storytelling fest!

Assignment: Tell a Tall Tale

1. Read one or more tall tales. Select one you like and find a brief segment in that story to tell the class.
2. Identify your book, author and segment by writing a sentence or two for the teacher to avoid duplications.
3. Practice your story segment on anybody (outside of class).
4. Limit yourself to five minutes, practice a lot, and then present to the class!

Example: *Paul Bunyan, Lumberjack* (from an account by Roberta Feuerlict in the book *The Legends of Paul Bunyan*)

Before Paul Bunyan became a lumberman in Maine (or Michigan or the Northwest), he was a schoolboy who had terrible problems because of his size. He was so big that he needed four desks to write on and his neck was so long that his head was always stuck up the chimney of the schoolhouse. His books had to be pulled to school one at a time because there was only room for one in the classroom. Paul couldn't write with ordinary pencils because they got caught under his nails. To make a pencil the right size, he had to pull up a tree and sharpen the end. He was always in trouble with his teacher . . . .

******

Paul was always a good eater for his age. For a light lunch he would eat three sides of barbequed beef, enough potatoes to fill a wagon, twenty cherry pies, and ten gallons of apple cider. When his stomach was empty, the growling sounded like a pack of grizzly bears!

Paul's pet ox, Babe, weighed 10,000 pounds. His feet were so big that his footprints made the holes for all the lakes in Wisconsin and Minnesota. Can you imagine what the lumberjacks fed him?

GA1082

The following books are only a few of the rich collections of tall tales, short stories and anecdotes about American folk heroes available in the library.

Tall Tale America, Walter Blair
American Tall Tales, Adrien Stoutenberg
The Rainbow Book of American Folk Tales & Legends, Maria Leach
Whoppers, Tall Tales and Other Lies, Alvin Schwartz
Davy Crockett: Frontier Hero, Walter Blair
The Legends of Paul Bunyan, Roberta Feuerlict
John Henry, Ezra Keats
The Ghost of Peg-Leg Peter and Other Stories of Old New York, Moritz Jagendorf
New England Bean Pot, Moritz Jagendorf

Some folk heroes to look for are Davy Crockett, Daniel Boone, Annie Oakley, Paul Bunyan, Tony Beaver, Pecos Bill, Old Stormalong, Joe Magarac, Mike Fink, John Henry, Johnny Appleseed, and many, many more!

Remember:
Tall tales are different than other humorous stories because tall tales are characterized by the most outrageous exaggeration.
Notice with what kindness we avoid the use of the word *lies.* Just think about the modern fisherman who says, "I caught a fish that was *this long,*" and every time he tells the story the fish gets longer.

Attention Storytellers:
The art of storytelling is alive and well. There are storytelling festivals taking place all over America. If you become intrigued with this traditional art form and are in search of more information, write NAPPS (National Association for the Preservation and Perpetuation of Storytelling), Box 112, Jonesboro, Tennessee 37659.

Taped Mystery: Creative Listening

Plan ahead for the sounds you will record on a tape recorder. The sounds should be strong sounds that can be identified and are evocative, such as a dog barking, a door slamming, a vacuum, the dishwasher, a power saw, a car pulling out of the drive, pounding, laughing, footsteps . . . . Ten sounds on a cassette should be adequate for creative listening. On the assigned day each student should be ready with paper and pencil. As students listen carefully to the mystery sounds on the tape recorder, they list them, trying to identify them accurately. A bell or other signal will separate each sound to help organize the listening experience. The students must try to identify the sounds as best they can and then string them together in a written mystery plot based solely on what they think they heard. Listening to the tape twice will make it possible to account for everything that was recorded. Do not share your impressions! More venturesome souls may want to provide dialogue to create a more lively thriller.

Volunteers may read their stories aloud to illustrate the possible variations in this creative listening process.

GA1082

Telephone Code: a Memory Aid

If you look at a telephone dial you will see groups of three letters assigned to a number. Sometimes it is a problem trying to remember some phone numbers. You may want to help yourself remember numbers by using a memory technique called a mnemonic (knee-mon-ic) aid. Experiment with the letters on the dial and try to make a seven-letter word or several small words from the phone number you choose. If it seems impossible to do, try to make a nonsense word that you can pronounce like *klonerz* or *gabluck* or *trowsax*. Can one of your classmates make a word out of a phone number which stumped you? Remember that phone numbers have seven digits. Make a list of your important phone numbers and code them into words!

Use this code.

1 (Sorry, you will have to use 1.)
2 ABC
3 DEF
4 GHI
5 JKL
6 MNO
7 PRS
8 TUV
9 WXY

Touch Tone

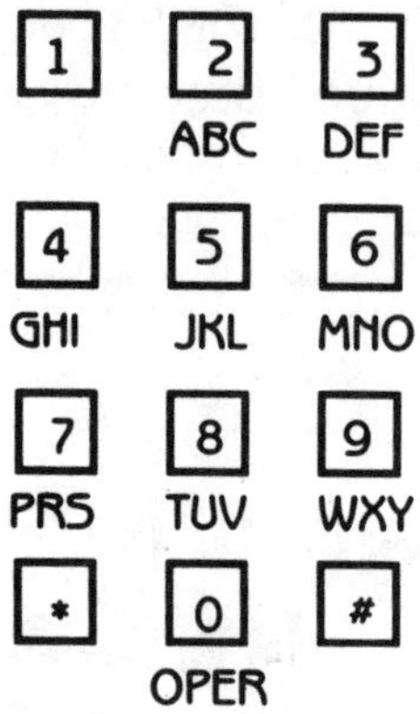

1	2 ABC	3 DEF
4 GHI	5 JKL	6 MNO
7 PRS	8 TUV	9 WXY
*	0 OPER	#

home _____

grandparent _____

father's work _____

aunt _____

other _____

best friend _____

mother's work _____

cousin _____

school _____

******

Change these words back to their phone numbers.

A M E R I C A

_ _ _ _ _ _ _

L I B R A R Y

_ _ _ _ _ _ _

G O O D B O Y

_ _ _ _ _ _ _

P I C T U R E

_ _ _ _ _ _ _

N U M B E R S

_ _ _ _ _ _ _

S A D S A C K

_ _ _ _ _ _ _

GA1082

Ten Thousand Ways to Write a Story

You probably will not believe this, but it is possible to generate ten thousand (yes, 10,000) story ideas using the following method. Brainstorm four lists under the headings:

I. Hero
II. Place or Setting
III. Villain
IV. Problem or Conflict

Decide on ten items for each list. Record the choices on paper as the students choose their own *current* heroes, villains, settings and conflicts. When the list is complete, write or tell a story by filling in the blanks in the narrative. Make one choice from each list. The complete list may be duplicated and given to each class member. In this way the story may be created orally or written. If there are ten choices in each column, there are $10 \times 10 \times 10 \times 10$ possibilities which = 10,000 possible combinations. Start with any column in any order and make random choices. A less ambitious enterprise can be managed by reducing the number of columns and/or items.

As each selection is made, the narrative is to be fleshed in with other details.

For example:

Muscle Man received a phone call in the dead of night. He knew the muffled urgent voice belonged to Mr. Goodheart, a respected citizen of Anytown. The voice begged him to rush to *Spike's Gym* on the edge of town. When he arrived, the doors were bolted shut, but in the illumination of the basement light he saw the profile of his old enemy, *Evil Eva!* Sparks flew from the tips of her crimson fingernails as she obviously *Cast a Magic Spell* on the hapless Mr. Goodheart.

How will the story end? It's entirely up to you! You may want to expand your choices by adding a fifth list entitled *V. Happy Endings.*

GA1082

I. Hero

Muscle Man

Crash Gordon

Lone Stranger

Handsome Hulk

Flash Fireball

Stella Strongarm

Tillie the Hun

Bella Brain

Officer Eagle-Eyes

Dauntless Dawg

II. Place or Setting

The zoo at night

A deserted house

A sausage factory

Spike's gym

A submarine

An amusement park

A closed department store

The edge of a cliff

A damp cave

A glass elevator

III. Villain

Grendel

Lester Loutish

Savage Sam

Terrible Tork

Rock Rotten

Evil Eva

The Smarm

Bayo Wolf

Heinous Hal

Gert Gagger

IV. Problem or Conflict

They would not believe the story.

Cast a magic spell

Running out of air

The place was flooding.

Chased by howling dogs

Fell in a vat of oil

Released from a cage

Lost in space

The power was cut off.

Surrounded by the enemy

V. Happy Endings

(Your choice)

140

Thumb Thing to Think About

We humans are lucky to have hands with opposable thumbs. Our thumbs can be moved against the fingers to help us grasp things and perform many complicated tasks. This short and thick first finger is different from the other fingers because of its greater freedom of movement. We seldom think about how remarkably well we are put together! To demonstrate the importance of this opposable finger, we will design a thumbless survival test. Tape your thumb to the palm of your hand. Try to perform ordinary activities without the use of that finger. Work with a partner who is not all taped up. Think of activities to perform while your partner takes notes on this experiment. Write your observations about life without a thumb.

Oops, sorry,—you can't write!

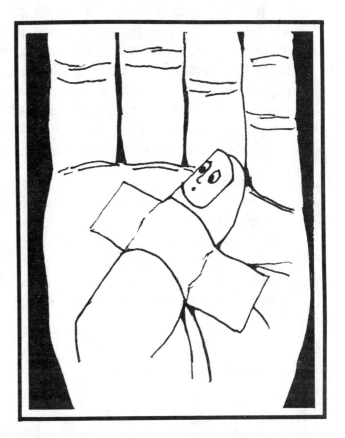

Time Capsule: Items for History

The Anytown Historical Society is planning to build a time capsule to be buried under a marble marker on the school grounds. The capsule is to be opened one hundred years from now and will be a source of important historical information for people in the future.

To communicate information about the time in which you live, the society has asked you and your classmates to make a list of items to be put into the capsule. You will want future generations, who open the capsule, to know something about:

1. the clothes we wear
2. our educational system
3. the food we eat
4. our technology (machines, appliances, etc.)
5. our money system
6. the practice of medicine
7. homes and shelters
8. religions that are observed
9. books, newspapers, libraries
10. recreation
11. farming, business, industry
12. war and peace
13. politics

With the class, decide what should go into the capsule. Give your reasons for each suggestion. How will you explain what the items are and what they were used for? Add any categories of your choice.

GA1082

Time Warp

The following statements (such as, "everyone was bald") describe situations as if these conditions were really true. The big question being asked here is: If these things are true—what else is true in that time and place? Add three facts to any statement of your choice that would expand and explain the setting of that time and place in history more completely. Your story "fillers" should make sense and help complete the picture. Think big! Think future! Think universal—war, politics, science, changes in nature caused by humans!

This is a very effective oral exercise for class participation.

Example:

Everyone was bald—

A strange pollutant had found its way into the water supply of Hard Luck, Kansas. At first only the men were affected. When the women and children began to lose their hair, there was great alarm.

(The speculation should be large in scope. The response to the "bald statement" should be more than "there were no combs.")

1. Fully prepared meals appear in the Food Scope by pushing a button on a Compu-Menu . . .
2. All cities in America are underground . . .
3. Any story you want to hear appears on a giant screen in your house. The characters and animals can step out of the screen and enter your living room. You can smell, touch, and interact with everything which becomes real . . .
4. Reading and writing is against the law . . .
5. Humans no longer have the weapons to wage war . . .
6. There are floating space environments complete with plants, animals and people which never come back to Earth . . .

Title Tellers: Synopsis

The students will collect and record all of the strange sounding book titles they have read, heard about, or seen in the library or on book lists. Call this a title search. Make selections from children's books or young adult books. Students pretend that they know what the story is about. Create a story synopsis which would logically fit one of these unusual titles. The class may work on one title, several titles, or the students may choose one for each individual. Remember, you can only summarize a story for a book you have not read. The teacher may read some of these productions and some students may decide to read the book to see what the story is really all about!

Some suggested titles could be:

1. *How to Eat Fried Worms* by Thomas Rockwell
2. *A Hero Ain't Nothing but a Sandwich* by Alice Childress
3. *Pardon Me, You're Stepping on My Eyeball* by Paul Zindel
4. *The Cat Ate My Gymsuit* by Paula Danziger
5. *The Eyes of the Killer Robot* by John Bellairs
6. *This School Is Driving Me Crazy* by Nat Hentoff
7. *The Pistachio Prescription* by Paula Danziger
8. *Chitty, Chitty Bang Bang* by Ian Fleming
9. *Charlie and the Chocolate Factory* by Roald Dahl
10. *Blubber* by Judy Blume

GA1082

Tongue Twisters

A tongue twister is the term that describes a sentence, a phrase, a rhyme or a paragraph which uses clusters of similar beginning consonants that are almost impossible to say *together* correctly. These selections are designed to twist the tongue, no matter how hard you try to keep things straight. They are funny, challenging and wonderful, but there is a rule that must be followed: you must say the twisters quickly and at least *three times*. Study them, practice them and recite them in front of the class if you are sporting enough to try. Laughter is absolutely permitted! After you have tried some of these old standards, you may include others you have heard or made up yourself.

1. Black bug's blood.
   Black bug's blood.
   Black bug's blood.

2. Unique New York.
   Unique New York.
   Unique New York.

3. The sixth Sheik's sixth sheep's sick.
   (repeat 3 times)

4. Rubber baby buggy bumpers.
   (repeat 3 times)

5. Bad black bran bread.
   (repeat 3 times)

6. The bottom of the butter bucket is the buttered bucket bottom.
   (repeat 3 times)

7. Try fat flat flounders.
   (repeat 3 times)

8. There's no need to light a night-light
   On a night like tonight;
   For a night-light's just a slight light
   On a light night like tonight.

9. Susie's shirt shop sells preshrunk shirts.
   (repeat 3 times)

10. Round and round the rugged rocks the ragged rascal ran.
    (repeat 3 times)

11. Theophilus Thistle, the successful thistle-sifter, sifted sixty thistles through the thick of his thumb.

12. Which rich wicked witch wished the wicked wish?
    (repeat 3 times)

13. Six thick thistles stuck together.
    (repeat 3 times)

GA1082

Tremendous: a Word Probe

First, the word *TREMENDOUS* is written in large letters on the chalkboard. Look at it very carefully. Take your time. Using the letters in the word, you will begin to see smaller words inside *TREMENDOUS*. Now, write it down on your paper and see how many words can be extracted from the letters. You may only use exactly the letters you see (not more) and put them in any order. Who can find the most words? What are those words? Who has earned the top score? If you haven't found seventy words, you haven't tried hard enough! Can you think of another word that is as tremendous for this game of skill?

Key:

Some examples of words found in *TREMENDOUS* are mend, end, do, us, trend, men, ten, net, sun, one, den, done, so, some, nut, met, sour, sound, mound, mouse, outer, meter, demon, tender, rest, rent, round, rend, teem, douse, dust, send, sender, muster, seen, seed, route, rude, dour, sour, duster, ester, steer, stern, sear, seer, dote, roust, reed, deer, red, doe, toe, store, dent, use, user, under, true, deem, toes, sermon, stove, note, notes, rude, ton, tune, tuner, stem, stern, teen . . .

Twenty Questions

Ask everyone in class to think of a very interesting character from the present or past. Ask for one volunteer to come up and respond to questions from the class as if he were that character. Everyone will be in search of the name of that person. Only twenty questions may be asked. If the identity of the person has not been discovered, the volunteer reveals it. Choose another student to come to the front of the room and repeat the process. Listen carefully to make sure all questions are answered accurately. The class members, at their seats, should take notes as the questions are answered so that a profile begins to emerge from the answers. Don't waste time on items which have already been answered!

Samples of questions to be answered "yes" or "no":
1. Are you a woman or a man?
2. Are you still alive?
3. Are you involved in politics, entertainment or sports?
4. Are you African, American, European or Asian?

Phrase the question in such a way that you get the most information. If you ask whether the person is dead or alive and the volunteer says, "Not exactly," that means you will have to rephrase your question. (Perhaps the person is a character in a book and, therefore, is not actually dead or alive.)

Be flexible about rules of the game. They should be made to respond to the needs of the group, which does not always mean the game will be easier!

145

GA1082

Vocabulary Word Drama

This activity will work with vocabulary words which (a) can be dramatized (b) are of special interest to the students, or (c) are currently part of their studies. Many words are mastered by students because they are unusual sounding, are delicious to say, are funny or unaccountably fascinating. Instead of the usual routine of using new words by writing them in a sentence, this technique involves drama to demonstrate the definition of a word.

1. Duplicate the word list for everyone.
2. The teacher writes the vocabulary words in sentences on slips of paper. Underline the "new" word to be defined.
3. All slips are mixed in a box. Pairs of students will pick one slip at random.
4. Each pair of "actors" looks at the sentence, finds the definition in the dictionary, and decides privately on a strategy to dramatize the vocabulary word, as suggested by the sentence.
5. The pair reads the sentence aloud to the class but will leave out the vocabulary word. They will then dramatize the word. Given the variation in imaginative interpretation, it might go like this:
    Actor I: I'll take this blouse, hat, shoes, slacks, socks, scarf, wallet . . ."
    Actor II: Can you afford all this?
    Actor I: Money is no object when I'm shopping.
6. The class, reading from the vocabulary list, guesses the word from the sentence and the drama.

"When Heather buys clothes she is *extravagant*!"

- The fans were *belligerent* to the team. (What did they say or do?)
- My neighbors *carp* at me all the time. (How?)
- Teach me to *dribble* a basketball. (What will you show me?)
- I could tell she was a *demure* girl. (How did she act?)
- That little fellow is a *martinet*. (How did he act?)
- They will choose a class *valedictorian*. (Who is that?)
- The *boredom* of the group was obvious. (How did they show it?)

Design your own challenging vocabulary sentences!

GA1082

Wacky Want Ads

The classified ads section of your daily newspaper is one of the most interesting sections in the paper. It is like a marketplace with offerings of goods, services and practical information. If you want to buy a bike, trade your ice skates, find a job, locate a family to adopt your kittens, locate a lost puppy, look through the classified ads. When you are writing an ad, the idea is to make it interesting and catch the attention of the reader. Because ads are listed alphabetically, some people may start an ad like this: An absolutely astonishing bargain! Remember, too, that you will be charged for each letter and for the number of days the ad appears. First, look carefully through the want ad section. Find a strange or interesting ad to share with the class. Now write a wacky want ad for something you want to buy, sell, or trade.*

FOR SALE cheap. Little brother, nonstop talker. Eats constantly. Cries without reason. Places blame on older brother. Good for laughs. Best offer. Will deliver. Call Sue 145-3424.

An ad in the classified section costs $7.50 a line with thirty characters for each line. Calculate the cost of your ad. Use this form to send your ad to the classified section.

The first line is only twenty-four characters including space (the first two words are capitalized). All remaining lines are thirty characters.

Please start my ad _____

Check enclosed ☐   Bill me ☐

1																													
2																													
3																													
4																													

Name _____ Phone _____

Address _____ City _____ Zip _____

Suggestions:
Could you really use:

1. A good athlete to join your team
2. A neat person to keep your room clean
3. A dog who will run all your errands
4. A brain that will do your homework

---

*Greta Lipson and Bernice Greenberg. *Extra! Extra! Read All About It! How to Use the Newspaper in the Classroom.* Carthage, Illinois: Good Apple, Inc., 1981.

GA1082

Weather Map

A weather map is astonishing to behold for the sheer volume and intensity of information it includes. Use the weather map of your local newspaper. As a class effort, start to process and detail the kinds of data presented for the reader. On the chalkboard list the general information presented on the weather map as it is selected by the students. Using the map as a source, the opportunity for questions and answers is almost unlimited. How many details do you observe as you examine the map?

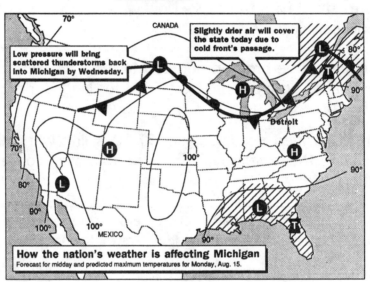

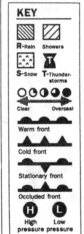

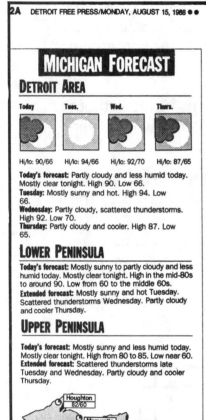

2A DETROIT FREE PRESS/MONDAY, AUGUST 15, 1988 ● ●

WEATHER

MICHIGAN FORECAST

DETROIT AREA

Today	Tues.	Wed.	Thurs.
Hi/lo: 90/66	Hi/lo: 94/66	Hi/lo: 92/70	Hi/lo: 87/65

Today's forecast: Partly cloudy and less humid today. Mostly clear tonight. High 90. Low 66.
Tuesday: Mostly sunny and hot. High 94. Low 66.
Wednesday: Partly cloudy, scattered thunderstorms. High 92. Low 70.
Thursday: Partly cloudy and cooler. High 87. Low 65.

LOWER PENINSULA

Today's forecast: Mostly sunny to partly cloudy and less humid today. Mostly clear tonight. High in the mid-80s to around 90. Low from 60 to the middle 60s.
Extended forecast: Mostly sunny and hot Tuesday. Scattered thunderstorms Wednesday. Partly cloudy and cooler Thursday.

UPPER PENINSULA

Today's forecast: Mostly sunny and less humid today. Mostly clear tonight. High from 80 to 85. Low near 60.
Extended forecast: Scattered thunderstorms late Tuesday and Wednesday. Partly cloudy and cooler Thursday.

AROUND THE STATE

Houghton 82/60
Marquette 84/60
S.S. Marie 80/57
Escanaba 85/60
Traverse City 85/60
Alpena 84/59
Cadillac 86/61
Houghton Lake 86/60
Muskegon 88/63
Saginaw 88/62
Lansing 88/63
Flint 89/64
Grand Rapids 90/66
Detroit 90/66
Kalamazoo 91/67
Jackson 90/66

High/low temperature today

Low pressure will bring scattered thunderstorms back into Michigan by Wednesday.

Slightly drier air will cover the state today due to cold front's passage.

CANADA
Detroit
MEXICO

How the nation's weather is affecting Michigan
Forecast for midday and predicted maximum temperatures for Monday, Aug. 15.

KEY

R—Rain   Showers
S—Snow   T—Thunderstorms
Clear   Overcast
Warm front
Cold front
Stationary front
Occluded front
H High pressure   L Low pressure

TRAVELER'S FORECASTS

City	Tue. Sky	Hi/lo	Wed. Sky	Hi/lo	Thu. Sky	Hi/lo
Boston	◑	93/72	◑	87/68	R	85/69
Chicago	◑	98/74	◑	95/71	◑	97/76
Los Angeles	O	87/66	O	92/70	O	88/68
Miami	T	99/76	T	96/74	T	97/70
Minneapls	T	88/69	T	87/72		NA
Milw'kee	◑	90/67	◑	89/72		NA
New York	T	94/71	O	92/74	T	93/73
Wash'ton	◑	95/70		NA		NA

LAKE FORECAST

Erie: West winds at 15 to 20 knots, waves 2 to 4 feet.
Huron: West to northwest winds at 15 to 25 knots, waves 2 to 4 feet.
Michigan: Northwest winds at 5 to 15 knots, waves 1 to 3 feet.
St. Clair: West to northwest winds at 10 to 20 knots, waves to 2 feet.
Superior: Northwest winds at 10 to 20 knots, waves 1 to 3 feet.

SUN AND MOON

Full	4th qtr.	New	1st qtr.
8/27	9/2	9/10	8/20

Sun rise/set: 6:40 a.m./8:35 p.m.
Moon rise/set: 9:35 a.m./9:49 p.m.

WEATHER FACTS

The temperature has stayed at or above 65 since July 27. That's the longest streak of 65-plus readings in 67 years. In 1921, the temperature in Detroit did not fall below 65 for 30 days, from June 21 through July 20.

Compiled by Allison F. Webster and Genie Klingler. Forecasts by Bruce Smith, University of Michigan Department of Atmospheric, Oceanic and Space Sciences. Weather Facts by Michael Betzold.

ALMANAC

TEMPERATURES

	Hi/Lo	Cooling degree days
Sunday *	92/77	20
Saturday	92/72	17
Normal/Today	82/60	6
Record/Today	97/46	19
Total/month	—	224
Departure/month	+137	+125
Total/season	—	875
Departure/year	+579	+407

PRECIPITATION

Sunday *	.01
Saturday	none
Record/Today	1.28
Total/month	1.33
Departure/month	-.06
Total/year	11.58
Departure/year	-8.35

* Through 5 p.m.; not included in month and year total.

HOURLY READINGS

7 p.m.	90	5 a.m.	78	3 p.m.	90
8 p.m.	88	6 a.m.	79	4 p.m.	91
9 p.m.	85	7 a.m.	78	5 p.m.	87
10 p.m.	83	8 a.m.	78	6 p.m.	88
11 p.m.	82	9 a.m.	80	7 p.m.	89
Mid.	70	10 a.m.	83	8 p.m.	87
1 a.m.	80	11 a.m.	85	9 p.m.	86
2 a.m.	80	Noon	87	10 p.m.	84
3 a.m.	79	1 p.m.	89	11 p.m.	82
4 a.m.	79	2 p.m.	88	Mid.	74

RECENTLY

Date	Hi/lo	Date	Hi/lo
8/8	93/67	8/11	90/73
8/9	92/74	8/12	93/71
8/10	87/71	8/13	92/72

HIGHS AND LOWS

U.S. high: Phoenix, Az., 113
U.S. low:
Michigan high:
Michigan low:

THE NATION

City	Sky	Hi/lo
Albany	T	92/65
Albuq'que	◑	92/68
Amarillo	◑	94/67
Anchorage	O	62/52
Asheville	◑	85/66
Atlanta	◑	91/72
Atlantic C	O	83/71
Austin	◑	95/75
Baltimore	O	97/75
B'mingham	◑	95/72
Boise	◑	83/50
Boston	◑	94/73
Brownsville	◑	94/77
Buffalo	◑	83/65

City	Sky	Hi/lo
Burlington	T	86/64
Char'ton SC	R	92/75
Char'ton WV	◑	94/71
Charlotte	◑	91/71
Cheyenne	◑	88/58
Chicago	O	94/73
Cincinnati	◑	93/70
Cleveland	O	89/67
Col'mbia SC	◑	92/71
Col'mbus Oh	◑	91/68
Dallas	◑	103/79
Dayton	◑	92/68
Denver	O	94/64
Des Moines	◑	103/74
Duluth	◑	88/65
El Paso	◑	93/69

City	Sky	Hi/lo
Fairbanks	R	62/50
Fargo	O	96/70
Flagstaff	◑	80/50
Hartford	◑	93/70
Helena	◑	85/55
Honolulu	O	90/76
Houston	O	95/74
Ind'apolis	O	95/72
Jackson	◑	96/73
Juneau	◑	65/48
KansasCty	O	99/78
Las Vegas	O	100/72
Little Rock	◑	97/75
LosAngeles	O	82/62
Louisville	◑	96/75
Memphis	O	97/78

City	Sky	Hi/lo
Miami	T	89/76
Milwaukee	O	92/78
Minn'polis	O	96/75
Nashville	O	97/73
N.Orleans	◑	91/75
New York	R	93/75
Norfolk	◑	93/75
Ok'ma City	O	101/77
Omaha	O	98/73
Orlando	T	91/73
Philadelphia	R	94/74
Phoenix	◑	106/84
Pittsburgh	◑	95/70
Portland Me	R	84/66
Portland Or	◑	75/54
Providence	◑	91/72

City	Sky	Hi/lo
Raleigh	◑	92/71
Reno	O	80/40
Richmond	O	95/72
Sac'mento	O	86/56
St. Louis	O	98/76
St Pt/Tampa	T	90/76
Salt Lake	O	92/66
San Antonio	◑	96/76
San Diego	O	75/65
San Fran	O	72/56
Seattle	O	69/54
Spokane	O	78/50
Tucson	T	99/76
Tulsa	O	101/79
Wash'ton	O	97/76
Wichita	O	104/75

CANADA

City	Sky	Hi/lo
Calgary	●	68/50
Edmonton	R	64/52
Halifax	R	68/57
Montreal	●	79/68
Ottawa	●	79/68
Quebec City	R	68/59
Regina	◑	84/61
St.Johns		NA
Thunder Bay	O	84/61
Toronto	◑	86/72
Vancouver	R	66/54
Victoria	R	66/54
Whitehorse	O	68/41
Winnipeg	O	91/63

THE WORLD

City	Sky	Hi/lo
Amsterdam	O	77/61
Athens	O	100/75
Bangkok	O	91/77
Barbados	◑	87/82
Beijing	R	77/68
Beirut	O	91/75
Belgrade	O	97/68
Berlin	O	77/54
Bermuda	●	91/82
Brussels	O	72/54
Buenos Ar	R	57/53
Cairo	O	99/73
Cop'hagen	O	63/54
Dublin	●	68/57

City	Sky	Hi/lo
Frankfurt	O	81/52
Geneva	O	86/64
Helsinki	O	66/54
Hong Kong	R	79/77
Jerusalem	O	88/68
Jo'burg	O	70/43
Kiev	O	84/64
Lima	●	61/55
London	O	73/59
Madrid	O	95/63
Manila	●	91/79
Mexico City	●	72/55
Moscow	O	75/63
Nassau	●	91/73
New Delhi	●	88/77
Paris		NA

City	Sky	Hi/lo
Rio	●	77/59
Rome	O	93/64
San Juan	R	89/75
Santiago	●	54/39
Seoul	O	93/79
Singapore	R	81/75
Stockholm	O	68/64
Sydney	O	62/51
Taipei	R	91/79
Tel Aviv	O	88/75
Tokyo	●	88/79
Vienna		NA
Warsaw		79/63

U.S., Canadian forecasts are today's. World readings are from two days ago.

*Reprinted with permission of *The Detroit Free Press,* Detroit, Michigan.

GA1082

Weather Rap

4/4 Time

B-R-R-R-R

Get up in the morn-ing and I want to know

What the wea-ther's going to be be-fore I go.

Need to get the pa-per for the wea-ther re-port.

Check-ing out the tem-pera-ture, and things of that sort.

Look-ing at the di-a-gram for pre-cip-i-ta-tion;

Rain-y wea-ther com-ing down all a-cross the na-tion.

Part-ly sun-ny af-ter-noon, it's stay-ing warm and breez-y.

Get-ting up to nine-ty-three, you bet-ter take it eas-y.

Chance for an af-ter-noon thun-der-show-er.

Winds blow-ing south-er-ly ten miles an hour.

Sun's going to rise at six fif-teen.

Then at nine p.m. it's going to leave the scene.

Read-y for the wea-ther now, I know the score.

WHEW

*Reprinted by permission of Harriet Goldman, Southfield, Michigan, © 1988.

GA1082

Windchill Factor

On some mornings the weather person on TV reports that the temperature is 25° outside but then goes on to warn us that we had better bundle up because the "windchill factor" is –4°. You know this report is accurate, and you pay close attention to it especially if you have to walk a long way to school. But what does this all mean?

Have you ever felt colder than the thermometer indicates? This is not just your imagination. It could be the windchill factor, which means that the combination of the wind velocity and the temperature together increase the feeling of cold.

To find out how cold it really is, the chart below will help you find the answer. This chart is an example of one used in a cold climate. For example, if the actual thermometer reading is 20° and the wind velocity is 10 miles per hour (MPH), the equivalent temperature, considering the windchill factor, is 2°.

If the actual thermometer reading is 20° and the wind velocity is 30 miles per hour (MPH), then the equivalent temperature, considering the windchill factor, is –18° (below zero).

You might live in a warm climate where "windchill" doesn't apply. What reports of natural conditions in your region do not apply to people in other areas?

Windchill Factor
Actual Thermometer Reading

Wind Velocity in MPH	35	30	25	20	15	10	5	0	–5	–10
				Equivalent Temperature						
0	35	30	25	20	15	10	5	0	–5	–10
10	21	16	9	2	–2	–9	–15	–22	–27	–31
20	12	3	–4	–9	–17	–24	–32	–40	–46	–52
30	5	–2	–11	–18	–26	–33	–41	–49	–56	–63
40	1	–4	–15	–22	–29	–36	–45	–54	–62	–69
50	0	–7	–17	–24	–31	–38	–47	–56	–63	–70

GA1082